Flavio

FLAVIO

GORDON PARKS

W · W · NORTON & COMPANY · INC ·

New York

First Edition

Library of Congress Cataloging in Publication Data

Parks, Gordon
    Flavio.

    1. Silva, Flavio da.   2. Handicapped children—
Brazil—Rio de Janeiro—Rehabilitation—Biography.
3. Rio de Janeiro—Poor—Case studies.   I. Title.
HV890.B72R56   362.7'1'0924   [B]   77–16544

ISBN 0 393 08806 5

1 2 3 4 5 6 7 8 9 0

For Leslie Campbell Parks

photographs follow pages 92, 144 and 186.

Foreword

As a photojournalist I have on occasion done stories that have seriously altered human lives. In hindsight, I sometimes wonder if it might not have been wiser to have left those lives untouched, to have let them grind out their time as fate intended. The outcome of two such stories still troubles me—Flavio da Silva, a Brazilian boy and his destitute family for whom this book is written, and the Fontenelles, a broken black family of ten, trapped in the cold and hunger of a brutal Harlem winter. The da Silvas and the Fontenelles lived across the world from one another, but they shared the same tragedy, a private tragedy but one at once very public—and I became caught up in their struggle to survive it.

After the Fontenelles' story was published in March, 1968, the family, with the money I requested from *Life* magazine and that contributed by its readers, was able to move into a comfortable little house on Long Island. There was new furniture, a front porch, grass and fresh air, and a good school nearby. The unemployed father was promised a job. An entirely new world had suddenly raced in upon the luckless Fontenelles and swept them away from the filth and chaos of their Harlem tenement. The oldest boy left prison swearing off dope forever. The mother and father, their four daughters and as many sons, were happy. I was happy for them. I visited their house regularly to try and help make the transition as smoothly as possible.

Then at three o'clock one morning several months later, fire destroyed the house, the father, and Kenneth, a younger son. In minutes, death and horror had replaced their happiness. Several Christmas Eves later I visited what remained of the family. The Fontenelles were scattered all over Harlem—all except the oldest boy, who, along with another brother, was back in prison. Three of the girls, aged from twelve to sixteen were, according to their mother, "on the streets." She had not seen them for three months. Only she and a five-year-old son shivered alone in the cold tenement apartment. There wasn't much I could say to Bessie Fontenelle as I left her. She stood, I remember, at the top of the stairs waving goodbye, saying finally what I could not bring myself to say, "Merry Christmas." Very weakly, I had called back to her, "and a happy New Year."

That night I thought, not for the first time, that I should have left them alone instead of hanging on to push them toward some remote or improbable dream. But the choice was never one I bothered to consider. The condition of anyone hopelessly ensnared in such misery and poverty could only be helped, I thought, by its exposure in such a great magazine. From the outset of each assignment to its very end, I reported objectively. But in the end, my emotions, which are by nature subjective, took over. Disguising these emotions in objective clothing I dug deeper and deeper into the privacy of these lives, hoping, I realize now, to reshape their destinies into something much better. Unconsciously, I was perhaps playing God. I hold a fierce grudge against poverty because I was so desperately poor when I was young. But accusing my past is hardly the answer. There is, I want to believe, a personal need to recognize the right of every man to live a reasonably decent life. Flavio da Silva's story was published in *Life* Magazine in March, 1961. Its outcome, which was essentially different, is narrated on the pages to follow.

gp

Flavio

One

It was burning hot. The noon sun cooked the mud-rot of the damp mountainside. Curlings of steam rose with the stench of garbage and human excrement clogging the open sewers that snaked down the treacherous terrain. José Gallo and I rested in the shade of a jacaranda tree halfway down Rio de Janeiro's infamous Catacumba favela. Around us and stretching far below, their tin roofs shimmering in the heat, was a tangled maze of shacks. But far off, to our right, a lagoon shone like a jewel set in dark-green foliage. In the far distance gleamed the white buildings of the rich oceanfront. It was my first day on the brutal slopes of the "hill." My thighs and loins ached. Now I was finding that even the descent was cruel.

I first caught sight of the small boy as he climbed unsteadily toward us, breathing hard, a five-gallon tin of water rocking on his head. He was horribly thin, naked but for his ragged pants.

13

His legs looked like sticks covered with skin and screwed into two dirty feet. He stopped for breath, coughing, his chest heaving as the water slopped over his shoulders and distended belly. I had seen many like him that morning on the way up, all with the same sullen stare of hunger and hopelessness. Death was all over him, in his sunken eyes and cheeks, in his jaundiced coloring and aged walk. He might have passed forgotten, just another starving child, half-alive, suffering his way up a narrowing path. But suddenly, with the jerky movement of a mechanical toy, his head twisted sideways to us and he smiled. Caught in a moment of awkward pity, we found ourselves unable to smile back. Then suddenly he turned and went on up the hill. I touched José's arm, and slowly we began to follow him.

I thought for a moment about the details of the *Life* assignment in my back pocket: "Find an impoverished father with a family of eight or ten children. Show how he earns a living, the amount he earns a year. Explore his political leanings. Is he a Communist or about to become one? Look into his personal life, his religion, friends, his dreams, frustrations. What about his children—their schools, their health and medical problems, their chances for a better life?"

Now, watching the frail boy, bent under his load, scaling the steep hill above us, finding such a father seemed irrelevant. The image of this child, I felt, might say more about poverty than a dozen poor fathers. Whenever he stopped to rest, we stopped to observe him. When he finally turned into a tiny shack near the top of the mountainside, he had become the subject of the story I had come for.

It was a leaning, crumbled place of odd plankings and rusted tin, nailed together wherever the materials chanced to meet. The boy had left the door ajar, but José knocked softly. From inside we could hear the fretful babblings of many children. José knocked again, louder this time.

"*Silencio! Silencio!*" a thin voice screeched in Portuguese. The door was snatched open and there stood the boy with the same deathly smile, gripping under his arm a naked baby who bawled and kicked. He whacked the baby across its bare rump and his smile widened. Then he rattled off something to us in Portuguese.

"He's asking us in. He says his name is Flavio," José said. Both of us managed a smile this time, and we went inside. The boy screamed at a younger boy whom I assumed to be his brother. He tossed the baby on the bed between two whimpering little girls, emptied the tin of water into a large milk can, and motioned for us to sit down. There were only two boxes and the sagging bed. José had seated himself on the corner of the bed, and I had just straddled a box when two more girls burst into the shack, screaming at one another. The larger one, about Flavio's size, began pounding on the smaller one, who looked about eight years old. Flavio stepped in to part them, only to receive a glob of spit in his face from the larger girl, who then fled back out of the door. Flavio wiped his face, smiled, and began to explain, with José translating.

"These are all my brothers and sisters." He pointed them out to us. "That's Mario, the bad one. That's Luzia, who thinks she's pretty. And that's Albia and Isabel on the bed with the baby."

"What's his name?"

"Zacarias. He's the youngest and I'm the oldest. Maria, the one who spit on me, is next to me. I'll get her for what she did. Batista is my other brother. He's at the bottom of the hill with Poppa and Mamma."

The interior of the shack was a pathetic place. It consisted of a small room, about six by ten. Its grimy walls were a patchwork of misshapen boards with large gaps between them. Through them one could see other shacks below, propped against the mountainside. One glassless window looked out over the depressing slope. The floor, rotting under layers of grease and filth, caught hot shafts of sunlight slanting down through holes in the tin roof. Several planks were gone from the floor in one corner, offering a hole large enough to swallow Zacarias. The bed, at one end of the room, was partially covered with a ragged gray blanket that was stiff with dirt. A broken baby crib stood next to the bed, and in the middle of the room was a table held together with wire. At the opposite end of the room stood the stove, a makeshift affair made from the rusted, bent top of a discarded gas range which rested on a foundation of bricks. A square piece of tin underneath it was meant to catch the hot coals that had burned large holes through the floor. On the stove stood a badly dented teakettle and two cooking pans charred black from open flame.

Flavio started a fire and soon its fumes brought tears to the eyes of the children. He began coughing violently as a bluish haze spread over the interior of the shack.

My strange language set me apart. "Americano, Americano," a child would whisper. "Si," I would answer, and they would shy away with grins and laughter. For the first hour they stood around eyeing me, pulling at my pockets and touching my camera. Now and then one of them would poke his finger into my ribs or pinch my arm, and await my reaction.

Maria returned to the shack after a while, but Flavio seemed to have forgotten the spit in the face. "Stir the beans," was all he said to her. As she began stirring the pot, she watched us, mischief glinting in her eyes. She was very pretty and knew it. She wore a baggy gingham dress that dropped several inches below her knees. She kept hitching the skirt up with her free hand, tightening it in one motion around her hips. Her hair, swept into a matronly bun, contrasted oddly with her eleven-year-old face.

Mario, sharp-nosed and angry-eyed, sat on the floor. Something was bothering him. A tear hung from the lid of one eye, and he pounded the floor viciously with an iron bar. "Stop it, fool," Flavio shouted. Mario's jaws tightened and his eyes burned into those of his older brother. "I mean it," Flavio shouted, shaking a bony fist. Mario lifted the bar defiantly, but Flavio snatched it from him and thumped his head with his knuckles. Now the smaller boy pounded the floor with the palms of his hands, his eyes shut tight in anger.

Attempting to ease things, I started a language game. Pointing at the side of the shack, I shook Mario and said, "Wall, wall." He didn't understand at first, then José prompted him. "*Ingles*, wall; Portuguese, *paredes*." I touched the door. "Door, door, *Ingles*."

Now he caught on. "*Porta, porta!*" he hollered with sudden joy. Then they all gathered around and joined in the mimicking game.

I picked up a dust-covered book from the table. "Bible."
"*Biblia! Biblia!*"
"Ankles."
"*Artelhos! Artelhos!*"
"Neck."
"*Pescoço! Pescoço!*"
"Face."
"*Rosto! Rosto!*"
"Belly."
"*Barriga! Barriga!*"
"Knees—legs."
"*Joelhos e pernas! Joelhos e pernas!*"

Now they were all laughing, shouting, "*Artelhos! Pescoço! Rosto! Barriga! Joelhos e pernas!*"

Flavio was grinning, covering his ears with his hands, pleased perhaps to see them laughing together for once. "Quiet! Quiet!" he finally shouted. When, after a few minutes, silence fell over the room, Flavio grabbed a stubbly broom and began sweeping the floor. The straws kept falling out as he swept, and he just kicked them aside. "The more you sweep with it, the worst it gets," he complained. Jose quietly translated for me as Flavio spoke. Occasionally he went to stir the black beans, using a scorched wooden spoon from which he licked the drippings. Now and then he allowed the others a lick or two; then he added pepper and a chunk of rock salt. After he got the floor as clean as possible, he pitched what was left of the broom down through the open hole in the floor. Someone shouted a complaint from down below but he ignored it and reached for a mason jar filled with rice, pouring half of it into a dishpan of water. He picked out the inedible grains and flicked them expertly through the same hole. Suddenly he looked up at his brother Mario who was stretched across the bed. "Mario, you lazy pig, go move the trash from the front!"

"Fuck you!" Mario snapped, leaping toward the door.

"What?"

Mario ran out with Flavio chasing him, but Mario, being the faster of the two, got away. Flavio hobbled back to his rice. "He's a bad one, a real bad one," he said, smiling. A growl, then a terrifying cry came from outside. Flavio scurried out ahead of us to find Mario sitting on a boulder rocking back and forth clutching his leg and crying.

"What's the matter now?" Flavio hollered, snatching his brother's hand away to inspect the leg.

"That damned dog bit me!"

"Aha, it's good enough for you, you lazy pig." He turned to Maria. "Hurry and get the alcohol—hurry." When she brought it back, he shook some on the wound. Mario howled.

"Quiet! Quiet!" Flavio shouted. "I bet you bit the poor dog first." Now he took Mario by the ear. "Come on. Get going and get that trash like I told you." The sulking Mario, more frightened than hurt, meekly obeyed this time.

Flavio returned to his rice and washed it with care, although the dirt from his hands blackened the water. Next he scooped out the grains and transferred them to a battered saucepan. But even the dirty water wasn't to be wasted; every drop carried from the bottom of the hill would get full use. He tossed in a chunk of lye soap and ordered each child to wash. After they had finished, Flavio splashed the water over the floor and, dropping to his knees, he scrubbed the rotting planks until the black suds soaked in.

The hardest and hungriest days of my early life had not prepared me for the favela of Catacumba. The poverty in New York's Harlem, on Chicago's South Side, in Puerto Rico's El Fungito seemed pale by comparison.

Flavio left the shack just before sundown, saying he would be back shortly. "Don't let the beans burn," he cautioned Maria. "If Poppa beats me, you get it later." Maria, happy to get at the licking spoon, switched over and began to stir the beans. I noticed she had tied a rope around the loose dress, pulling the hemline well above her knees, tightening the folds about her slim hips which she coquettishly rubbed with the palms of her hands. She dipped out a full spoonful of beans and swallowed them, then slyly took another helping. Luzia watched out of the corner of her eye as she preened before a broken mirror. "I see you. I'm going to tell," she said.

Maria's eyes flashed in anger. "You do and I'll get you, you little bitch." Luzia threw a stick at Maria and ran out of the shack.

Zacarias, the baby, dropped off to sleep. Mario slouched in a corner and began sucking his thumb. The two smallest girls, Isabel and Albia, sat on the floor, clinging to each other with a strange tenderness. Isabel held onto Albia's hair as if she were about to pull it, and Albia clutched at Isabel's neck. They appeared frozen in an act of violence.

Flavio came back a half hour later burdened down with wood, dumped it beside the stove, rested a few minutes, then started on a second trip below for the night's supply of water. It was dark when he finally shuffled into the shack, groaning under the weight of the five-gallon tin. His body drooped with exhaustion. His face, no longer smiling, looked like an old man's. By now José and I could see that he was the one who kept the family going. In the closed world of that shack, tormented by the needs and bitterness of his hungry sisters and brothers, he was waging a hopeless battle against savagery and death.

By the time Nair and José da Silva came with Batista that night, José Gallo and I had become part of the family. Flavio had already told them we were there when he went for the water, but Nair appeared a little surprised to find me on their bed with her children leap-frogging over me: yet she seemed pleased that they were at least laughing. "Gorduun Americano! Gorduun Americano!" they shouted at her. She was a dumpy woman, swollen with another pregnancy. Her brown wavy hair, curled in sweat over her forehead, was swept back in a tight ball. She had a fine nose and no doubt had once been a handsome woman. Now a permanent sadness had settled into her face. She wore a long, crinkled black skirt and a faded gingham blouse that was buttoned only to where her stomach curved out with the coming child. Her heavy hands and forearms were noticeably whiter than the rest of her body, and her bare calloused feet had lost their shape for shoes. She acknowledged us silently with a shy, toothless smile. Zacarias scrambled off the bed and went to her. She took him up into her arms and began to rock him gently. Then she slumped upon a box, softly patting the child's behind. She seemed tired beyond speaking.

José, the father, viewing us with skepticism, managed a curt hello, then ordered Flavio to hurry up the dinner. Barefoot and dressed in baggy trousers and a faded blue shirt, he was a portrait of gloom. There was plenty of Indian in him. It showed in his smooth dark coloring, his sharp features, his black wire-straight hair, and his easy lope of a walk. His face brightened when he saw the children with some small change I had given them, but he confined himself to a corner where he sat on a box scowling at the holes in the ceiling. Batista, a handsome boy of about seven and considerably darker than his brothers and sisters, sat at his father's feet. He seemed less tormented than the others. He had the calm of a grown man. His hair was straight and dark like his father's; his eyes, warm-brown and deep set, looked upon you for minutes without blinking. Something, perhaps his calm, set him significantly apart.

Flavio scurried about like a scared rat, his quiet plainly expressing fear of his father's presence. When the dinner was ready, José da Silva, as head of the house, took his place in the center of the bed with his legs crossed beneath him. The others gathered around him on the bed. There were only three tin plates and Flavio filled them with the black beans and rice and set them on the bed before his father. Then José da Silva, using one of the two spoons he owned, began to eat first. He chewed for several moments, judging the taste, then gave the official nod for the others to start. They joined him, eating eagerly with their fingers. Flavio rushed about at his father's orders, bringing more salt or pepper, pouring water or coffee, breaking chunks of stale bread. Finally, using the top of a coffee can for his dish, he got himself some food. But now came the moment of embarrassment for him. He wanted to offer José and me some food, but he dared not with his father sitting there. So, hiding behind his father on the floor, he edged his rice and beans toward us, gesturing for us to take some. We refused and he smiled, knowing that the three of us understood.

Later we got down to the difficult business of obtaining permission from José da Silva to photograph his family. He hemmed and hawed for a long time, wallowing in the sudden and pleasant authority of the decision maker. At last he gave in.

"You can photograph us," he said with a toss of his head, "but you must show us in a good light."

"Could you tell us a little about yourself?" José asked.

He hunched his shoulders, crooked his head, and extended his arms as if to signal disgust. "But there's nothing to tell," he answered. "I'm a poor man with a wife and eight kids and no money to clothe or feed them. What else can I say?" He was reluctant to say more. But after some coaxing he explained that he was a *Nordestino*, a refugee from dirt-poor northeast Brazil. Now he sold bleach and kerosene in a tiny store he and Nair had built from orange crates and pieces of stolen lumber. "I make about twenty dollars a month. My wife brings in another five washing clothes at the bottom of the hill." This accounted for the strange whiteness of her hands and forearms. We had passed the line of washtubs earlier that morning where the favelados had been queued up for water at the only spigot at the bottom of the favela. José Gallo had pointed out three crude toilets that were meant to accommodate the thousands on the mountainside.

José da Silva had stepped to the doorway and looked up at the dark sky after making his decision. He didn't ask why we had chosen his family, nor did he seem to care about our motives. But his eyes and manner told us that he eventually expected something of us. Now, gazing sullenly into the night, he complained of his back. "It will take money for me to get well," he groaned. José Gallo and I caught his message. When we asked him what the next day's weather would be, he groaned again. "Bad, bad—the pains in my back tell me so."

It was late. Zacarias, the baby, slept contentedly against the softness of his mother's stomach. Mario, Luzia, and Maria had collapsed in a heap with their limbs spread across one another. Albia and Isabel were sprawled in a crooked embrace, snoring loudly. At the top of the bed, apart from the others, lay Batista with his knees drawn up to his chin, his body curled as though he still slept in the womb. As we were saying goodnight, Flavio fell into a spasm of violent coughing. For a few moments his lungs seemed to be tearing apart. Suddenly, I wanted to get away as quickly as possible. It was a cowardly reaction, but the bluish cast of his skin beneath the sweat, the coughing, choking, and spitting were unbearable.

In our eagerness to outdistance the sound, we hurried down through darkness, trying not to look like strangers. "This is no place for outsiders after sundown," José said softly. The maze of dark paths, the steep, endless jungle of shacks made it an ideal hideout for criminals who used the night to rob for money and food. Once there had been police quartered in barracks below, José explained, but they were accused of raping a prisoner's wife and daughter. In revenge, the favelados had come one night with flaming torches, burned the barracks to the ground, and chased the police out for good. The only protection the favelados had now against the thugs and toughs was that which they sometimes mustered between themselves. Even to the police, the favela was off limits at night. They would come in packs, and only by daylight, to hunt down the criminals who hid there. As we moved past groups of men huddled in the shadowed darkness, it was disturbing to realize that, if we were attacked, there would be no help.

Halfway down, three men came up the path toward us. They were weaving from drink. As we passed them one grabbed my arm and demanded a cigarette. But José pulled me on. It was good to reach the bottom of the hill where there were street lights. "Don't ever come here at night alone," José cautioned me. "If you get caught up there after dark, it's best to stay at the Da Silva's until morning."

We drove slowly around the lagoon toward the city. The large white buildings began to rise against the mountains in the distance. That world we had just left behind in the musty dark now seemed like a bad dream.

My hotel on the Copacabana waterfront seemed surreal after a day in the Catacumba favela. When I entered, the lobby was crammed with people dressed in formal attire: a party was going on in one of the ballrooms. With the stink and dirt of the favela in my clothes and nostrils, I hurried to the elevator, hoping no other passengers would be aboard. But just as the door was closing a beautiful girl in a white lace gown stepped in. I moved as far away as possible. Then her escort, resplendent in his dinner jacket, jumped in and swept her up in an embrace that lasted until they got off at the next floor. Neither of them even realized I was there.

My room appeared oversized when I entered it. The entire Da Silva shack would have fitted into one corner. I ordered a steak, vegetables, salad, wine, and crepes suzette. Then I drew my bath. No bath had ever felt so good. I propped my feet up on the edge of the tub to drain the blood from my swollen ankles and soaked in the hot suds for thirty minutes.

The steak came and it was good. But in the middle of it, I suddenly thought of Flavio's black beans and crusty rice. I thought of the sick boy sleeping in a broken bed with eight others, coughing, straining for air in the muggy night. My appetite vanished, and I pushed the table away and went out to my balcony. The cost of my dinner alone would have brought considerable happiness to that miserable shack. How wonderful it would have been if I could have greeted them the following morning with meat, fresh vegetables, fruit, and new clothing! But there was nothing I could do about it. Flavio's predicament was my story. Still, the thought of allowing the Da Silvas to go on like this even for another day depressed me, although they had existed in this manner for years. I finally dropped into an uncomfortable sleep, knowing that I had to get the boy Flavio to a doctor as quickly as possible.

Two

Fog hung over the favela when we approached it early the next morning. José stopped the car, and we got out and observed Catacumba through clouds moving in the distant grayness. From our vantage point far away on the city side of the lagoon, it reminded me of the lovely blue hillsides along the coast of southern France. As we looked, a cloud broke over the mountain of Corcovado, widening and billowing, with the sun bursting through. Then suddenly the giant concrete figure of Christ loomed up into the radiant opening, its great arms extended over the valleys below, its massive back turned upon the slopes of Catacumba.

"Cristo Redentor," José explained sleepily.

I stood entranced for a long time, neglecting to photograph it. Then another cloud swept in and the figure disappeared.

The next time, I told myself, I'll shoot first and become entranced later.

"We can wait for a while. It may happen again," José said. And he went back to the car and sat down, while I stayed in the open with my camera ready. Normally José acted as a business manager in the Time-Life Bureau in Rio. He was assigned to Flavio's story because his time was more flexible than that of the regular reporters, and since he was fluent in English and Portuguese he could also act as my interpreter. Perhaps it was his official position at the bureau that prompted him to wear a suit and tie, even on the hottest days on Catacumba. Today he looked as if he were on his way to church. José was about forty, slow and soft-spoken. He was tall, slightly stooped, and very thin; his black hair seemed at odds with his sallow skin. He hated the sight of the favelas and considered them a source of embarrassment to his country. His arms lazily flailing the air, José often condemned their existence. "They are like cancers and just as incurable," he would say wearily. "But what can you do? We Brazilians worry about them, but you just can't worry away 700,000 favelados. The government has to do something concrete, something solid about it."

We waited for half an hour for Cristo Redentor to appear through the fog again, but it never did; so we decided to drive on.

The square at the entrance to the favela was bustling with hundreds of favelados when we entered it. It wasn't the type of square one sees in towns and villages around the world, but more like the large and barren backyards in the eroded rural areas of the southern states, with one huge, unfriendly, and impoverished family going about their chores. Long lines of people waited at the water spigot, and the women, unable to buy soap, were using stones to beat the dirt out of their clothes at the washtubs. Mothers screamed at the children, who chased each other through the garbage and sewage ditches. Men with lumber, sides of tin, tool boxes, picks and shovels, and other burdens important to their existence needled their way in and out of the noisy throngs. Dogs fought, their snarling and barking cutting into the constant chatter of the washwomen. From a loudspeaker high on a pole at the side of the square, a Brazilian samba blared, lending a bizarre carnival-like atmosphere to the scene. The odor of woodsmoke mixed with the stench of rotting things hung in the air. And through the mist that curled lazily over the higher paths, we saw columns of other favelados climbing like ants, with wood, sacks, and water cans on their heads.

Before long we spotted Nair bent over her tub. She saw us about the same time, stopped, smiled, and wiped away the sweat with her apron. We asked for her husband, and she pointed toward a tiny shack about five yards off to her right. This was José's store, where he sold kerosene and bleach. Built of odd scraps of wood, it was about twelve feet long and six feet wide. On one side there was an opening with a counter where he sold his wares. This is where we found him, sitting on a box, dozing. Sensing our presence, he awoke and greeted us with a nod; then he started complaining about his back again. "It kills me, kills me. I go to the doctor but they do me no good— because I don't have money. Talk, always talk and a little pink pill that does no good. What is to become of me?" he moaned. A woman came with an empty bottle and placed it on the counter. He got to his feet and filled it with bleach. The woman dropped some money on the counter and as she walked away, José da Silva's eyes watched the movement of her backside until she was out of sight. Then he started to complain of his back again.

"How much do you average a day?" José Gallo asked.

"Seventy-five cents. Maybe a dollar on a good day."

"Why aren't the older kids in school?"

"School? The teachers are crazy. They tell kids stupid things.

I don't want my kids around them. Furthermore, I don't have money to buy them the right clothes for school."

"Has Flavio seen a doctor lately?"

"That's the clinic right there," he said with a hostile shake of his head. "They are mad at me because I built my store in front of their place. I won't tear it down so they won't do anything for me or my kids. Just talk, talk, talk, and pink pills."

I couldn't work up much sympathy for José da Silva or his aching back. I wanted to go up to the shack to see Flavio; so I nudged José Gallo and we started off just as the sun blazed through the muggy air. Before we got halfway up, the heat was burning into our shoe soles. We climbed slowly, stopping now and then for a rest, following the trail of mud, jutting rock, and slime-filled holes; passing one rotting shack after another propped up against the slopes on their shaky pilings. A dead cat covered with maggots lay on a garbage heap. I tried to hold by breath until we reached better air but every few feet the open sewer was clogged with human excrement and more garbage. Most of the favelados we passed on the way up were barefoot, and the evils of this soil on which they walked day after day showed on their legs and feet. I stopped to watch one little girl whose legs were raw with running sores. José saw me wince. "This is nothing," he said. "There are over 700,000 of these people in the hills around Rio. You see the same thing in all of them."

Farther up we recognized Flavio climbing ahead of us, weighted down with firewood. When I lifted my camera to focus on him, some fierce grumbling erupted from a group of men who were sharing a beer beneath a tree a few feet away.

"They're threatening you," José cautioned. "Keep walking. Most favelados think the camera is an evil eye that brings bad luck. You have to be careful. One man was beaten nearly to death a while back. They smashed his camera and threw him out into the street." We kept climbing.

Flavio had stopped. He was observing something coming toward him from a connecting path. A man was descending with a small coffin on his head. A woman with a small child followed him closely. Their faces were expressionless as they inched their way down. They passed, and as Flavio turned to watch, he caught sight of us and waited. We took the wood from him. He protested, saying he could carry it, but he gave in when I hung my camera around his neck. Then he went on ahead of us, beaming at everyone who passed us.

The Da Silva shack looked even more squalid than it had the day before, and there was just as much chaos when we entered it. I wondered how, in such a weak condition, Flavio could face this each day—the fighting, the whimpering, and the filth. But there wasn't a trace of irritation on his face. When the others saw him with the camera about his neck, they looked at me in astonishment, thinking perhaps that I had given it to him. Now they wanted the camera, but Flavio held them at bay by lining them up and pretending to take their picture. It was a mistake, for I spent the next hour protecting the lens from their inquisitive little fingers.

Lighting the fire to warm leftover beans, Flavio turned to us. "Someday," he said, "I want to live in a real house on a real street, with good pots and pans and a bed with a sheet . . ." The smoke rose and curled up and out through the wall cracks and ceiling. Then an air current forced it back into the shack, filling the room and Flavio's lungs with the fumes. Before he could speak again, a coughing spasm caught him. It continued for several minutes until again his skin turned blue beneath viscous sweat. I handed him a cup of water, but he waved it away. Kneeling now on the floor, his stomach tightened, his chest heaved, and his veins throbbed as though they might burst. It was frustrating to watch and not be able to help. Strangely, none of his brothers and sisters seemed to notice. They never stopped whatever they were doing. Perhaps they had seen it too often. After about five minutes it was over, and he got to his feet smiling as though it had all been a joke. He wiped the sweat from his face and ordered Maria to undress Zacarias. It was the baby's day for a full bath.

"But there's rice in the bath pan," Maria protested.

"Dump it in another pan, then—and don't waste any." He still breathed heavily.

Maria had been plastering her hair with a dirty gray grease. She wiped her hands on her hips and took the little ragged garment off Zacarias. Knowing he was about to be bathed, Zacarias began to cry. Irritated, Maria gave him a solid smack on his bare bottom. Mario slipped up and gave her the same. Then a free-for-all started. The baby ended up on the floor with Maria and Mario slinging fists at each other. Flavio waded in and Mario got it in the eye. Then Mario ran from the shack calling Flavio a dirty son-of-a-bitch.

"It's always the same, always the same," Flavio said apologetically.

"Son-of-a-bitch! Son-of-a-bitch!" Mario kept screaming from a safe distance.

After Flavio fed the others black beans and coffee, they calmed down. Now was a good time, I thought, to get him to the doctor in the clinic below. José agreed. "How about going to see the doctor , Flav?" he asked.

"It's okay but you better see Papa first. Maybe he won't like it."

"Wash up and put on something clean. We'll go down and talk to your father."

"It's okay-fine with me," he answered. He took the wet dish rag and rubbed a layer of dirt off his arms and legs. Then, going to a bundle of clean rags, he pulled out a buttonless top that resembled a shirt and put it on pridefully, as though it were a new suit. There were no clean pants so he kept on the ones he was wearing when we first met the day before. Maria was put in charge and we started off.

Jose da Silva put up less resistance than we had expected, and after a few moments of thinking things over, he threw up both hands. "Do as you wish. Nothing will come of it in any case. Nothing."

José Manuel da Silva was always taciturn, often morose and difficult, but Nair looked upon him as a good husband and provider. With enormous effort he had built their shanty on the favela hillside, and then while working on a construction job he had been hit by a plank that had fallen from five floors above him. Injured and incapacitated, he had collected a monthly pension only twice from Brazil's then corrupt and nearly bankrupt social security system.

Scrabbling for a living, he picked up scrap wood and put up a stall near the favela wash fountain, selling soap and kerosene. The twenty dollars a month he earned barely kept his family alive, and he had lost heart. "I am tired to death all the time," he told José, "always struggling to get nowhere." Bitterness and hopelessness had become an ingrained part of his attitude.

The favela clinic stood just across the ditch from José da Silva's store. It was somewhat larger than most of the shacks surrounding it. I thought that perhaps it had once been someone's home, for there was a porch where the overflow of patients waited in the open. After about an hour, we worked our way inside to a small barren room filled with favelados. Mothers sat on wooden benches along the wall with children whose limbs and faces were covered with open sores. Babies suckled at their mother's breasts. Some patients stood savagely eyeing their neighbors. One bright-eyed black girl of about fifteen sat on the floor just inside the doorway playing with a white rag doll. Her legs were shapeless and strangely flattened beneath her. A closer look revealed that she was paralyzed from the waist down. An aged blind couple sat holding hands. The man's ear seemed to be in an advanced state of decay, and he kept dabbing at it with a crusted, dirty cloth. "Cancer," I thought. Both of them were ragged and barefoot, and her hands and feet were hopelessly stiffened from arthritis. Wrinkled and gray, they sat in their double darkness looking as though they awaited some final sentence to be passed upon them. At times the room quieted to a murmur; then maybe a baby would scream, and all the others would suddenly explode into a wail of hunger and hurt.

Flavio sat nervously between José and me on the edge of the bench. "What will the doctor do to me?" he kept saying.

"We'll see," José answered. "We'll wait and see."

In all there were over fifty people waiting, looking like refugees fleeing some disaster. But for them there was no place to run. They were born into a catastrophe from which the only escape was death.

After another hour, when Flavio's turn came, he broke out in a sweat. But he ambled through the door ahead of us and smiled at the nurse. If she noticed his smile she didn't let on. In such a place of misery, smiles were rare and unexpected. There was only one doctor, a large, crew-cut, beady-eyed man with a look of impatience about him. I began to dislike him intensely as he examined the body of the frightened boy. ("Open your mouth. Say 'Ah.' Jump up and down. Breathe in. Breathe out. Take off all your clothes. Bend over. Now stand up. Cough. Louder. Cough.") He went about the examination with cold efficiency. Then, turning to José and me, he said rather sadly in English, so Flavio wouldn't understand, "This poor little chap has just about had it. I've seen him about. He's been in once before. He's living on borrowed time." My heart sank. Flavio was smiling now, not having understood. The doctor had spoken with such passion that I was instantly ashamed for having formed such a hasty and biased opinion of him. His apparent coldness, I realized, was aimed at the conditions that spawned such a body. He instructed the nurse to give Flavio some pills and a bottle of cough medicine. Then he motioned José and me into a private room. "I hardly know where to start. This is Da Silva's kid, isn't it?"

"Yes."

"What interest do you have in him?"

"We just want to help in some way."

"Well, I'm afraid you're late. His whole body is wasted with bronchial asthma, malnutrition, and, I expect, tuberculosis. His heart, his lungs, his teeth are all bad." He paused a moment and wearily rubbed his forehead. "And all this at the ripe old age of twelve." A smile of disgust came to his face. "Eighty percent of the children in these hills around Rio are just as bad off. Only about ten percent don't have tuberculosis. Last year ten thousand of them died from dysentery alone. All of them have some form of malnutrition. But what can we do? You saw what's waiting outside. Every day it's like this. There's hardly enough money to buy aspirin for them. Only a few of the wealthier people help or care about these people. They keep the clinic going. Without them, we couldn't open tomorrow." He was quiet for a moment or two, thinking, trying to give us some hope. "Maybe the right climate, the right diet, and constant medical care could pull him through. Here, this poor lad is finished. He might last another two years or so, maybe not. I'm sorry I can't promise more." We thanked him and left.

"What did he say?" Flavio asked as we scaled the hill.

"Everything's going to be all right, Flav. There's nothing to worry about. Absolutely nothing."

It had started to rain when we reached the top. A heavy mist hung in the sky. We looked up and there was the Christ figure with clouds swirling around it again. I said a quick prayer for the boy walking beside me. And, as if he had read my thoughts, he said, "Papa says "El Christo" has turned his back on us here in the favela."

"You're going to be all right."

"I'm not afraid of death but I worry about my brothers and sisters. What would they do?"

"Don't worry, Flav. You're going to be all right. Don't worry."

The lie weighed heavily on us. But what else was there to tell him?

From then on, each day was about the same; days of watching this sick boy in a hopeless struggle to help his family survive; days of cataloguing the moods, the tensions, the little happinesses and the big despairs, the constant hunger, the rare instances of sympathy and love. After two weeks it became increasingly difficult to know who I was and why I was there. The personal involvement, the impact of the overall tragedy of Catacumba, had disjointed my reasoning. My own family, the magazine for which I worked were, at times, a little more than blurred memories. Now people along the steep paths were getting to know me. "*Bom dia,* Americano," they would say. Through their gradual acceptance of me, I was beginning to feel like one of them. I became more careless about my personal safety.

Reality returned one morning as I climbed alone toward the Da Silva shack. I suddenly found myself surrounded by several young toughs. They were threatening me and pulling at my camera. Covered with goose pimples, I spoke quietly and firmly. "Out of my way," I said, and pushed through their little ambush.

As I started up the hill a voice stopped me. "Have trouble, Americano?" I turned to see a tough-looking, six-foot, jet-black sharpie leaning against a rock, dressed in tight blue jeans and a red shirt open to his waist. He wore sandals and peered at me through dark glasses. From his neck hung a rather splendid silver chain, from which dangled a leopard's tooth and a voodoo amulet.

"Nothing I can't handle," I answered.

"I speak American. I been to Baal-tee-more and Francisco on ship once. Work on cargo ship for year from São Paulo." He glanced at the young toughs who had stopped me. "They punks. You see me Americano. My name is Dantas. Dantas know how to handle punks." I started walking off. "Hey, Americano, you give Dantas cigarette?"

I just might need Dantas some day, I thought to myself. I reached in my pocket and pulled out a pack of Marlboros and tossed them to him. This pleased him and he flashed me a big smile. "Thanks, Americano. Thank you many many much."

In the early part of the third week, the New York office of *Life* cabled the Rio bureau. They were concerned about my silence as well as the assignment. I sat down outside the Da Silva shack after José had given me the cable and thought for nearly an hour, assessing the story as I saw and felt it, feeling that perhaps I had gotten too close to it. Would they think I was out of my mind, getting so involved with the problems of a boy instead of a father, as they had suggested? "To hell with it," I finally said to José. We went below to the city and I filed the longest cable of my life—all about Flavio and the awful favela of Catacumba. There was no word from New York for over forty-eight hours, and I became concerned. Then, on the third morning, a terse reply came:

CATURANI FOR PARKS FROM TIM FOOTE IT LOOKS LIKE YOU'RE ON TOP OF A GREAT STORY—FLAVIO SOUNDS TRAGIC BUT HE ALSO SOUNDS WONDERFUL—STICK WITH HIM AND KEEP US INFORMED—KEEP A DIARY— REPEAT KEEP A DIARY STOP BEST FOOTE

My first entry was made the next evening.

March 22, 1961

This morning I reached the shack at 7:30. Little Zacarias was crawling around naked in the filth outside.
Maria, Albia, and Isabel were swinging in a greasy
hammock hung across the room from one wall to the
other. Flavio was cooking black beans and rice for
lunch. The kids seemed glad to see me.

I stepped back to take a picture of the hammock and
upset the pot of beans. This sent them all into hysterics. Flavio, who because of his asthma and weak
lungs must satisfy his expression of mirth with a broad
grin, enjoyed the luxury of a real laugh until the strain
brought on convulsive coughing. He became so weak I
had to hold him. Later he scraped up the beans and put
them back in the pot.

We could almost see him dying now. Maybe next month,
next year. Who knows? Certainly he wouldn't live out his
childhood. By now I had started buying food for the family.
One day I brought small presents for the kids—dolls for the
girls, small cars for Mario and Batista, and a fancy pocket knife
for Flavio. Until then, their only toy had been a discarded baby
carriage wheel which they pushed about with a stick. But when
word spread that the Da Silvas were getting large supplies of
food, jealousy grew amongst their neighbors. Suddenly, favelados who had once been friendly began making hostile com-
ments. José and I were not excluded. José da Silva didn't get
upset one bit about this; meat, greens, potatoes, bread, and
fresh milk were more important that a neighbor's scowl. But
Nair was deeply concerned. After Mario was beaten one day by
three boys, she started carrying a heavy stick. I tried softening
things by bringing small gifts to some of the other kids who

lived nearby, but this only made matters worse. The Da Silva
kids became jealous then and struck back at their small friends.
I was their private property. From then on, we brought food
up after dark or concealed it in my camera case.

March 23

Unlike Flavio, the other kids are unpredictable. I
am "Gorduun" to them now. Sometimes two or three
of them wiggle beneath my arms, grip my fingers
tightly, and remain so for several minutes. Still, it is
not surprising when one sticks me with a nail or pin.
Either act is committed with the same feeling. It is as if
they are testing my responses to their love or violence.
Nair, their mother, doesn't have time to give the love
they need—and the father seems incapable. So any
hand that touches with gentleness is dear. But to ig-
nore one of them for long is to abuse them. Their reaction is sullen anger or violence.

Maria was plastering her hair with the dirty grease
this morning. It was flecked with brown particles and
gave off a rancid odor. When I found out it was drippings from hog fat, I went below and bought her a bottle of perfumed hair oil. Immediately she washed out
the other and soaked her hair with the scented liquid,
grinning, sniffing, and combing as if she were about to
meet a handsome prince. She reached for Luzia's broken mirror to inspect her efforts but Luzia refused her,
spit at her, then me. Then, stomping my toes, she ran
from the shack. Maria skipped over to a pile of clean
rags, yanked out a wrinkled dress and put it on. Then
kissing me, she skipped out to let her less fortunate girl
friends smell her hair.

At half-past nine one bright, hot Saturday morning, a tri-
umphant voice bellowed over the loudspeakers, commanding

all favelados to come to the square for a "great political rally."
"Come hear *your* Senator, the great man *you* put in office! Be
here in one hour! Bring your problems! He's got the answers!
Don't miss it, my friends! He has wonderful news for you!"
The voice croaked off, and a jazzy samba spilled over the
mountainside. José and I inched through the gathering
crowd, searching for the elder Da Silva. We now referred to
him as "The King." We found him with a bunch of political
banners under his arm, backed up against the counter of his
store. A woman was harassing him, shaking her finger close to
his nose.

"It is a sin against God and humanity," she admonished,
"keeping your children out of school. You should be ashamed
of yourself." The King spotted us and fled up the hill past us
mumbling, "A crazy teacher, crazy, crazy." The woman spit at
his heels and strode off in another direction. José da Silva
began tacking the posters on nearby shacks, for which he
would collect twenty-five cents.

Punctually the Senator arrived, naked from the waist up,
his gray silk shirt flowing over his arms. A gold medallion
hung from a chain around his neck. He was a big, handsome,
moustached man with black, well-groomed hair. A pungent
odor of cologne hung over him. His stomach hung over his
belt. Now the samba had changed to a blaring martial air. He
came through the swollen crowd, smiling, shaking a hand
here, bending to kiss the cleaner babies here and there. Now
he stopped at the water spigot, a former campaign promise,
cupped his hands and filled his mouth with water; not swallowing, he spit it out. "Pure, pure water, fit for a God to
drink." He inspected the three toilets that had been scrubbed
down for the occasion. "There will be more of these—after
the next election," he promised, slapping his hip. Then he
pushed through the crowd and mounted the steps of the food
store facing the square and began his speech.

It was a speech that, if fulfilled, could have turned the Catacumba favela into a hillside paradise. If he were re-elected, there would be better housing, steps to the hilltop, more jobs, police protection, more toilets, more water spigots. Whatsmore, there would also be better schools, clinics, and enough medicine for everyone. "All this for you from a servant who has proved that he keeps a promise!" Except for a few on the fringes who applauded, the crowd was silent. "Disease and death must leave this hillside! And I will drive it out! My office is open to any and all of you whenever you have a problem. No one will be turned away at any time. I am your servant! I will serve you!"

After his speech, the Senator stepped down into a mass of complaints, and wiping his handsome brow, listened, took notes, and made more promises. Finally, an old lady pulled him from the crowd and ushered him up the hill. We followed. "My daughter is dead," she was wailing, "and no one will bring a certificate of death so we can bury her."

"How long has she been dead, my good woman?"

"Since yesterday morning. Now, you come and see."

The temperature was well over ninety, and I wasn't anxious to enter the shack that held the dead woman. The Senator, I imagined, was no more anxious. But in spite of the intense heat, the neighbors had kept the parlor of death reasonably cool. The sun had been shut off from the windows with sides of cardboard boxes. Pans of cooling water were at the head and foot of the bier of wooden crates. Two women, using large, leafy branches, fanned away the insects. A board about five feet long made the headrest. Two vigil candles in ash trays burned on each end of the board. Another candle burned at her feet. The pillow for her head and linen sheet used for a shroud were amenities few favelados received in life. These, the old lady told us, were lent by more fortunate neighbors. "There once was nine children," an old man cut in. "Now, with her gone, there's only six. The other three are with God. He was good enough to take them." A hand towel had been placed under the dead woman's chin and knotted at the top of her head to keep the mouth closed. And an extra box of candles lay on her chest.

The scent of the Senator's cologne did not sit so well here. He mumbled his blessing and promised to get a coroner to issue a burial certificate "as quickly as possible." He took the old lady aside. "You know," he apologized, "this is the week-end. More than likely, the coroner is vacationing." José and I followed him to the bottom of the hill, thinking maybe the Senator could help with Flavio. "I will be glad to do anything I can."

"We will come to your office tomorrow," I said hopefully.

"Not tomorrow, my friend. The wife and I leave for Paris in the morning. I have urgent business there."

The Senator kept his promise. The certificate of death finally came late that night and the dead woman was taken down the next morning at dawn. "She went to her grave un-smelling," a neighbor told us. "She was all bones with no flesh on her to rot. It's the meaty ones who spoil fast."

March 24

Flavio was daydreaming when I arrived today—looking out over the shacks, past the football field, the lake, and the great white buildings. Though he is twelve he has never been to downtown Rio. None of the kids have—not even to Rio's famous Copacabana Beach, which is only ten minutes from the bottom of their miserable world. I have promised Flavio to take him there. Maybe one trip outside will, if he lives, give him the incentive to get out of this. I may create a longing impossible to fulfill, but I think it is worth the gamble. When he is daydreaming like that, he feels

lonely. I stood watching him. After a while, not knowing just how to express his feelings, he walked over
and took my hand, rubbed his face against my arm
over and over again. Luzia is very pretty and must
know it. She licks herself clean like a little cat. She can
be surrounded by filth and emerge from it without a
blemish. It is remarkable how she manages this
against such odds. After I took pictures of her preen-
ing, she was especially intolerable to Maria. Today a
neighbor brought a fish which Maria had to clean. She
was knifing the guts from its belly when Luzia came
up and touched the tail.

Before Luzia could duck and I could focus my camera, Maria smacked her in the face with the messy
fish. Instead of tearing into Maria as I expected, Luzia
complained to Flavio. Maria sensed trouble and
started to run, but Flavio wrestled her arm until she
dropped the fish, then slapped her in the face with it.
Maria grabbed the knife and went for Flavio's back.
Dropping my camera, I grabbed her wrist.

Now I found myself in trouble as she wrenched free
and came slashing at my stomach with the knife. I
stepped aside, spun her about, and shook the knife
from her grasp. She dug her teeth into my arm but I
held her tightly for a moment. Then, to my surprise,
she looked up at me and wailed. "Mawny Gorduun!
Mawny, mawny!"

The favelados fought hunger, disease, and death from
sunup to sunset. And this fight had spawned a hatred in them
for anyone outside their tragic world. One day I saw that
hatred turned against a local television cameraman who had
been assigned to photograph me as I worked in the favela. To
shield the Da Silvas, I purposely took him to another section
where conditions were equally bad. He was a big man, blond,
broad-shouldered, and about six-foot-four. As I turned my

camera on the rubbish piles, children, and shacks, he followed close behind, filming my actions. Things went well
until we started down. A group of young toughs, looking
much the same as those who had once surrounded me, began
following us.

"Just keep working and walking," the cameraman said. He
sensed trouble. Then the toughs overtook us and began curs-
ing the cameraman. They pushed and shoved him from one
side of the path to the other, spitting on his face, his arms, his
hair, his legs and feet. Furious, I turned and cursed them.

"Keep moving," the cameraman cautioned. "Don't mind
me, just keep moving." It seemed ages to the bottom of that
hill. When we reached the street, I felt deeply ashamed to
have been spared their spittle. My dark skin had saved
me—and I wasn't very proud of it. We started across the
street. Two young favelados ran past us. There was a screech-
ing of brakes, a scream, but it was too late for the smaller one.
He was caught under the speeding car. His crumpled body
skidded to a stop on the hot pavement about a hundred yards
farther on. The car slowed for a moment, then sped away with
scores of favelados screaming after it. An angry mob circled
the dead child. Some cried, some cursed, others lit vigil candles and crossed themselves. Finally, someone brought a
sheet. It was white and embossed with fancy initials. A part of
some rich family's laundry, I suspected. When the blood
began to seep through the cameraman touched me and we
hurried away from the hostile gathering.

"That bastard never even stopped," I said.

"And it's good he didn't," the cameraman replied. "He
would have been killed on the spot. He'll report to the police
within a few hours. That's all that is required here in Rio." At
a safe distance we turned and looked back toward the savage
hill; the favelados were still streaming down to the dead child
below. Suddenly their hatred was more understandable.

When José Gallo and I arrived at the Da Silva's store the
next evening, José da Silva was cleaning Batista's face, preparing him for church. Little Isabel stood in the darkness scowling at me. I often thought of her as a bitter flower. Her days
were spent frowning and biting, kicking and crying. I tried in
every conceivable way to win a sign of affection from her. But
she had never once smiled. So I was surprised when she suddenly ran to me and threw her arms about my legs—only to
bury her teeth in them. I kept rubbing her hair gently, hoping she might soften under such treatment, but she just
kicked my shins. The next moment she let out a pained cry
and pointed to her foot. Lifting her to my lap, I groped for
whatever was hurting her. A thin, rusty nail had entered her
foot from the bottom and was protruding through the top. I
pulled once, twice. She screamed but the nail hadn't moved.
The third time I pulled with all my strength. It was out, and
my hand was smeared with blood. Her mother grabbed a bottle of raw alcohol and doused the wound, while Isabel gripped
my neck tightly. Then I set her on her father's counter. Her
mother's face was crumpled with concern. But her father
didn't bother to inspect her foot—even though he was less
than three feet away. A few minutes later I followed him and
Batista to church, watched them kneel together in prayer. I
wondered about his singular attachment to this boy. Was it,
perhaps, because Batista was the darkest one in the family?
Was it because he refused to share in the mischief and violence of his brothers and sisters?

March 27

It was unbearably hot today. The elder Da Silva,
looking more dead than alive, lay shivering and feverish underneath the crusty blanket. He squirmed beneath the covers groaning, "God, what's to become of
me? What's to become of me?" A huge black spider

crawled over his leg and little Isabel, standing nearby, watched until it reached his knee; then, doubling her fist, she smashed it. Her father shrieked, and his hand shot out and landed against Isabel's face. She stood crying beside the bed until Flavio took her to the stove, dunked some bread in coffee and pushed it between her lips. For a moment, she was quiet but then she started crying again. Suddenly, for no apparent reason, she walked over to Zacarias, the baby, and kicked him in the head. Then Luzia, in defense of Zacarias, shoved Isabel to the floor. Mario smacked Luzia, causing Flavio to intervene. In Mario's haste to get away, he plunged headlong into his mother who was entering the door. She grabbed him, cuffed him about the head, and he fell to the ground screaming, "What'n hell you hit me for?" Isabel, her sullen wet eyes on Luzia, sat gloomily in a corner. "Bitch! Bitch! Bitch!" she muttered. After cleaning her feet with stale coffee, Luzia went outside, doubled herself up on the ground, and began sucking her thumb. The mother sighed, picked up Zacarias and placed him on the table where she sat down and buried her head in her arms.

Gradually, after five weeks, I had grown used to the tension and despair that wracked the Da Silva family. But although I sometimes tried, it was impossible even to imagine myself forever trapped in this backwash of humanity. Reality always provided escape; I could get out whenever I chose to. And, for me, this made the imprisonment of the others all the more tragic.

I went one Saturday night to the hotel's sidewalk cafe for a drink. I sat there for a half hour watching the men customers bargain with young prostitutes who passed by, subconsciously comparing the lavishness of these surroundings to those in the

favela beyond the hill that separated the two worlds. A
slender girl with sad eyes approached my table. "Would you
like fun, Señor?"

"No."

"But it is very cheap."

"No."

"I need money for my sisters and brothers. They . . ."

"Here," I said, handing her about a dollar's worth of cruzeiros. Then I went to my room, changed into my work
clothes, and ignoring José Gallo's advice, I took a taxi back to
the Catacumba.

By then, it was past midnight. The driver realized I was a
foreigner. "Do you know where you are going?" he asked
when he let me out at the bottom of the hill.

"It's okay," I said. And he drove away. For a moment I
stood looking up at the dark mountainside, wondering, a little
frightened. Finally, I concealed my camera inside my shirt
and went in. The store on the square was still open and its
lights made the entrance less forbidding. But a third of the
way up I ran into the still, menacing blackness and realized
suddenly that José was right—this was indeed no place for
anyone after dark.

I climbed cautiously, passing a figure now and then, tens-
ing with each movement or noise that came. The climb
seemed hours longer than any I had made up this path before.
The fork running off to the Da Silva shack had been easy
enough to find in daylight, but in the blackness I suddenly
feared I had passed it. I started to turn back but confusion
gripped me. I had lost all sense of direction. Better to go on to
the top, where there would at least be a clearing to sleep in.
Furthermore, no taxi driver would think of stopping to pick
me up down at the bottom of the favela at this hour. I went
on.

As I started up the path a small animal scurried across my

foot; then a larger one, a dog, leaped from above. Then came the fierce screech of a cat, the brief sound of a death struggle, then quiet. Now I could make out the limp form of the cat hanging by its broken neck from the dog's mouth as he trotted past me.

Farther up, a man sat in the doorway of his shack rocking a child in his arms. A woman lay asleep on the floor just behind him. They were backlighted by vigil candles burning at the head of another makeshift bier. I slowed, seeing a child's face set in death under the flickering light.

"*Bom dia*," I said.

"*Bom dia*," he answered.

I didn't know how to express my sorrow further. One less cat to forage the garbage. One less child to face the cruel tomorrow.

"Hey you, Americano!" The voice had come out of the darkness. I tensed and looked toward the direction from which it had come. "It's me, Dantas. I meet you on hill the other day, remember? I been to Baal-tee-move and Francisco on ship once. Remember?"

I adjusted my eyes to the darkness. It was Dantas all right. He stood smoking by a tree. His white teeth gleamed through a big smile. I recognized the leopard tooth and voodoo amulet dangling from the chain around his neck.

"Good to see you, Dantas," I lied.

"Why you up this way so late tonight, Americano?"

"I'm lost, I guess. Which way to the Da Silva house?"

"Oh, you pass it down the way. Come, I show you."

"I started back down the path, but he grabbed my arm, nodding his head to our left. "No, that is the long way. We take short way over the hill. Come." We walked a few steps, then he stopped and took the cigarette from his mouth and offered it to me. The scent told me it was marijuana. I took it, drew the smoke in deep, and handed it back. The taste was

harsh, like the dried corn silk I used to smoke behind my father's barn when I was a kid.

"It is good stuff, hey, Americano?"

I lied again. "Good stuff, Dantas. Good stuff."

"You need some, Dantas got it. Cheap too."

The path narrowed between some rocks. Dantas motioned
me ahead. I didn't like the idea of walking ahead of Dantas in
the dark. I motioned him on. "After you," I said.

After about a hundred yards we came to a clearing where
three shacks hung on the cliffside. Dantas stopped and
pointed to the middle one. "That is mine," he said. "Come
take look."

"I have to get down to the Da Silva house."

"Just one minute. Nice place. You can see."

We entered, and for several uneasy moments I stood in
total blackness, a strong aroma of incense enveloping me as
the sound of Dantas's sandals moved over the creaking
boards. He struck a match and lit a candle. The dim glow
revealed a wall full of awful paintings, and they covered the
ceilings as well. There were black, purple, and red nudes,
pink and yellow dragons breathing fire, snakes and huge spi-
ders, and one painting of a black leopard covering a huge
black woman in a sexual act. Dantas smiled with delight as I
stared at the strange collection.

"Nice, huh, Americano? My woman and me paint them.
Cheap too."

I was about to answer when something moved on the floor
to my right. Looking closer I saw three boys, ranging from ten
to fourteen years old. They were sprawled on a mattress, fast
asleep.

"Your kids?" I asked.

Dantas laughed. "No, no, not my kids. They work for Dantas. They gonna be good *melandros* someday soon. I make
them good. Two, three year they be good *melandros*. I take

good care of them. I have a very good one name Concho two
year back. Best on hill. But he get killed by dirty pleeceman
who double-cross me. But Dantas get even one night a week
later. We catch him double-crossing again and we put the
blade to him right here." Dantas pointed to his stomach. I
wondered what a *melandro* was.

A soiled lamé curtain opened behind Dantas and a young
girl of about sixteen stood in the opening wiping sleep from
her eyes. She had a creamy skin and shoulder-length black
hair. She wore blue jeans but was naked from the waist up.
She observed me for a moment, then disappeared.

"My woman, Coreta. She work for me too, in bed on the
hill. Good woman." He shot me a sly glance. "You want
woman, Americano? Cheap. Only two Americano dollars for
all night, yes?"

"Nope. I've got to get down to the Da Silva house."

"Maybe sometime, huh?"

"Yep, maybe sometime."

We left and he walked me down the hill a few yards to the
Da Silva shack. I was amazed to find we were so close to it. I
had seen the path leading to Dantas's place, but I had never
ventured up it. As Dantas turned away I was tempted to ask
him what a *melandro* was, but then I thought better of it. In
the next moment he had slipped back into the blackness of the
mountainside.

Flavio was having another bad night. I could hear him
coughing as I approached the shack. I knocked softly and his
mother let me in. A strong eucalyptus scent filled the shack.
Flavio sat on a box in the weak light of a kerosene lamp inhal-
ing steam from a pan of hot water. All the others were asleep.
Nair's face was drawn and she slumped in fatigue. I motioned
her into bed beside her husband. Before lying down she
poured a small portion of clear liquid into a tin cup; then added
as much cold coffee. She stirred the mixture with her finger,
then put it to Flavio's lips. Grimacing, he drank it. When the

water cooled, I heated some more and held it beneath Flavio's face. He fell asleep after about an hour and I lifted him into bed beside the others. I wondered about the liquid Nair had mixed with the coffee. I tipped the bottle, poured some on my finger, and tasted it. It was kerosene.

At last I blew out the lamp and sat on the floor with my back to the wall. My feet and ankles were swollen again; so I removed my shoes and propped my feet up on a box to relieve the ache. The family's snoring rose and fell in uneven rhythms, punctuated now and then by Flavio's hacking coughs. The blue-black sky looked unreal through the cracks of the walls. I sat in the strange darkness watching the embers cooling and flaking into ashes, unable to find my place in such an experience.

Eventually I fell into a nightmare of sleep. The great concrete statue of Christ tumbled backward into the favela crumbling the hills and its shacks into a river of terror. There were coffins filled with garbage and human limbs. And it was Mario, not Flavio, who lay still upon another makeshift bier, in flickering candlelight. I finally awoke in a sweat. The luminous dial on my wristwatch showed four o'clock. Then I must have gone back to sleep, for the next thing I knew it was dawn. Flavio was already up, tiptoeing about, boiling the stale coffee from the night before. He was trying not to awaken me or the others. Later, when the others began to stir, he soaked hard chunks of bread into the coffee and placed them on a pan next to the bed. For each of them, including the baby, this was breakfast. I would bring them some cereal the next time I came. That morning I learned that the space left by the missing floor planks served as a toilet.

April 7

This was the day I had promised the trip to Copacabana Beach. When I arrived this morning at seven,

Flavio and Mario were already waiting at the entrance to the favela, waving and jumping excitedly. They made no attempt to clean up; so the dirt from the day before still covered their bodies. Except for their soiled, tattered pants, they were naked. I wanted to suggest that they wash up a bit, but their eagerness got the better of me. They scrambled into the back seat and pleaded for José to drive on. As we rolled through the valley of gleaming white buildings, Mario's hand closed tightly about Flavio's and the two of them sat closely together, wide-eyed and silent, in the center of the car seat, looking.

Suddenly the whole of the vast, curving waterfront and the thronged beach came into view. The car moved slowly along it.

"Look, look, look," Mario cried. Hundreds of multicolored umbrellas cast pools of shade over the blinding sand. Children of the same ages as Flavio and Mario ran about, eating, laughing, playing leapfrog, and flying large, colored kites.

"Flav," Mario said, turning to his brother, "is this here all the time?"

"Yes, yes, yes, of course," Flavio shouted.

At first the two were afraid to move about on the colorful, serpentine walks and the wide expanse of sand beyond. They were just feeling bold enough when a jet liner roared over from behind the building. They ducked and cringed. After the noise died away, they joined hands and warily approached the water. The first time a wave broke against their legs, they screamed and ran. But within minutes they were skipping joyfully and unafraid in the foaming surf.

Later they walked along gasping at the elaborately dressed windows of Rio's expensive stores. I brought them food but they were too excited to eat it. For once, their souls seemed hungrier than their stomachs. When it was time to go, they begged for one last ride along the waterfront. So we turned and circled while Flavio and Mario sat silently as we made a final sweep past the vision of beach and sea.

I was filled with confusion and guilt during my final days in the Catacumba. Flavio, like thousands of other children, would die as the doctor had predicted. His family and all those other families would sink deeper into the mire of that stinking slope. It seemed futile to believe otherwise. I could not help but compare the good fortune of my own children with the fate of these others. Fate might have so easily reversed the circumstances. I had told myself that Mario and Flavio's trip to the beach might stick with them, might give the incentive for their eventually escaping their miserable world. But I knew differently. I had exposed them to an impossible dream, and I would be leaving in a day or so.

I tried to be objective. The fact that I had become deeply attached to Flavio was irrelevant. After all, his real importance was not this personal bond, but the fact that he was the medium through which I could show the ugliness of poverty to millions of people. For a moment, I was like the man who is proud of his inability to shed a tear—free of any sentimental attachment to an experience. I would be a tougher, better reporter for this. That night I slept peacefully with my new resolve, only to have it shattered when we met Flavio on the upper path the next morning.

"Gorduun, Americano, *bom dia.*" He smiled brightly. His eyes twinkled when he saw that I held two sacks of groceries in my arms. He offered to carry one and when I gave it to him, his hands pressed into the sack to see what I had brought. Then he sniffed at the top. "Ah, meat, oranges, and coffee," he said, beaming his thanks.

Suddenly, the roar of a plane jerked his head upward, and we stood a few seconds watching the jet aircraft roar upward, its trails of vapor fleecing the cold air behind it.

"I go back to America tomorrow, Flav."

He seemed hurt. "You go to stay?"

"To stay," I answered, thinking for a foolish instant of his being up there beside me, then rejecting the thought as quickly as it had come.

"I would like to fly to America with you."

"Perhaps someday, Flav. Perhaps someday."

We both laughed at the thought of such a thing. Then we climbed silently to the shack.

When we started taking out the groceries, Flavio's brothers surrounded us, pushing and shoving one another, trying to see what we had brought. They gazed at the meat, vegetables, and fruit with a kind of sad gaiety. One would jump now and then, clapping his hands in joy. But when Flavio took out the lollipops, bedlam broke loose. Happiness momentarily filled the Da Silva shack.

José and I went to see the doctor again that afternoon, this time without Flavio. The doctor shook his head disconsolately and repeated, "Maybe several years in the right climate, with the proper medical care and diet, he could pull through."

He walked to the window and looked out on the cluster of shacks that leaned to within a few feet of the clinic door. "As I have already told you, he has already gone so far. It would take thousands of dollars, expert care, and the hand of God. I can't offer any encouragement. I'm sorry." We left him and waded through hundreds of others whose chances were no better than Flavio's.

We stopped at José da Silva's store. There were no customers, and he lay asleep on a large bundle of rags. Farther on, we passed Nair washing at the tubs. She exchanged smiles with us and continued to rub.

"What's a *melandro*, José?" I asked as we drove along later.

He turned and gave me his usual sleepy look. "A dirty crook who deserves to be shot," he said dryly. "They make crooks out of the poor kids on the streets and in the favelas. They sell women and dope and use the kids as go-betweens for stolen goods. They even teach them how to use knives and guns, They'd kill you for a couple of bucks. When the cops go up after them, they go up with a big force of men." I thought about Dantas and shivered. "The powerful ones run gangs in several of the favelas. They make trouble, then make the favelados pay them to protect them from that same trouble."

"Can't the police clean them out?"

"The police?" José scoffed. "The police are afraid of them, I tell you. Now and then the cops catch up to them and there's a big battle. Then the police and the *melandros* end up dead in a ditch somewhere."

We rode along for a while before José questioned me. "Why do you ask about the *melandros?*"

"Oh, nothing. I just heard someone use the word the other day," I answered. I couldn't bring myself to tell him that it was this guy named Dantas, who had been on a ship to Baltimore and San Francisco. José would certainly have thought I was an idiot.

José and I drove slowly to my hotel. We didn't say much. Flavio's story was finished.

April 9, 1961

With José, I said goodbye to Flavio and the family today.

"Gorduun, when do you come back?" he asked.

"Oh, someday soon, Flav," I lied.

"You come back to favela to see Flavio, yes?"

"Someday soon, someday soon."

Now I was telling myself that perhaps I could manage it in some way, even to take him out of this place. He walked with me to the car, rubbing my hand as we went. Then there was a scream and I looked back to see Maria chasing Mario up the hill with a stick. Flavio stood grinning as I pulled away.

"Come back to the favela, come back." He turned and hobbled back to the hill, and I lost sight of him among the jungle of shacks.

Three

The plane to New York took off at midnight. As we gained altitude, Rio, far below, sparkled like a jewel. Cristo Redenter, brilliantly bathed in flood lights, stood with its great concrete arms stretching mutely into the night. Behind it, somewhere down in the big blackness, was Flavio and his family. We banked steeply out over the ocean, then there was nothing but the glow of moonlight on the metal wings.

By three o'clock everyone was asleep and the plane's cabin was dark; only the persistent drone of the motors rose above the quiet. I was oppressively tired, but I couldn't sleep. The weeks with Flavio and his family had been an overwhelming experience, and I tried to shake my mind loose from it. I concentrated on what was ahead of me in New York, focussing on those things that would have to be done before Flavio's story could be properly presented to Ed Thompson, *Life*'s managing

editor. Nearly a hundred rolls had yet to be processed and con-
tact-printed on 8 x 10-inch sheets. From those sheets the very
best pictures would then be selected for blowups that would
convey the wretchedness of Catacumba. My tote bag held several notebooks filled with scribblings. The diary I had kept
would be reshaped and expanded from this material, which
would also provide the information for picture captions. There
was still a lot of work ahead.

As I contemplated the order in which I should do these
things, the depressing notion that Flavio's story might never be
published struck me. I quickly dismissed it as a ridiculous
thought. When it bounced back, a mild anxiety seized me—
perhaps with good reason. During those past weeks when I was
so caught up in Flavio's problems, the unpleasant image of the
rejection bin on *Life*'s 30th floor had often popped up before
my mind's eye. I had come to hate that bin. I remembered it as
always being filled to overflowing with stories that had been
written and laid out but would not make it that week to the big
Donnelly presses in Chicago, where the magazine was printed.
Many of them would never make it at all. There were, of
course, certain stories that deserved to be there, but there
were some awfully good ones sandwiched between the others.
The thought that Flavio's story might end up in that bin momentarily unnerved me. "It is impossible," I kept murmuring
to myself, knowing well, through personal experience, that it
was indeed possible.

Ten years earlier *Life* had sent me on a search for my childhood classmates. I was only sixteen when I had last seen most
of them; they were now scattered over a good portion of the
United States. The hunt took over four months. It was an interesting journey, but at times traumatic. Some of those childhood friends were doing fine; some had hit bottom. Finding
one in the high offices of state government, highly respected
and still moving upward, cheered me. Finding a once-beautiful

girl in a dismal big-city ghetto, dying a slow death from heroin addiction, left me despondent. Shortly after the story was finished I was assigned to the Paris Bureau for two years. It was there, on one joyous morning, that I received a cable from the New York desk:

YOUR WONDERFUL ESSAY ON YOUR CHILDHOOD CLOSED THIS WEEK FOR A COVER AND 12 PAGES— CHAMPAGNE TONIGHT—AND CONGRATULATIONS.

That evening my wife and I went to a good bistro on the Left Bank to celebrate. My wife hated champagne so we settled for a bottle of Beaujolais.

On the following day something *very* big happened to General Eisenhower, I can't remember just what, but in any case my "wonderful essay" wound up in that bin on the 30th floor. It stayed there for over a year. Then it was forgotten.

An extraordinary event—the death of a famous person, an earthquake, a declaration of war—could send your story to that bin. No photographer or writer at *Life* actually knew that his story was appearing in any particular issue until he saw it in that issue on the newsstand. Over the years, on rare occasions, the mammoth presses had been stopped so that some scheduled lead story could be scrapped and replaced by one held to be more newsworthy. Such a sudden switch sent the managing editor, and a substantial number of his staff, scurrying to Chicago. There, fortified with cold sandwiches and hard liquor, they produced in one sleepless night what it normally took them a week to write, edit, and lay out. It was an exorbitantly expensive operation, but it was the most effective way to vie with the capricious nature of news.

As the plane droned through the night I thought about how Tim Foote, a *Life* editor, and I had struggled to get what eventually became Flavio's story assigned. Tim had included poverty on the list of subjects he had proposed to write in a five-part series, *Crisis In Latin America,* for the summer of 1961. The subjects were: *The Menacing Push of Castroism, Bolivia—The U. S. Stake in A Revolution, Latin America—A History of Turbulence, Prisoners of Our Geography,* and *Poverty,* which I was assigned to photograph. *Life's* top editorial board had approved the series as early as February, but there was a serious catch. The board insisted upon my shooting only one photograph of poverty in seven separate Latin American countries. Both Tim and I objected vigorously to this because we felt that such an approach was far too impersonal. We preferred to confine the story to one situation, hoping that *Life's* readers could more easily relate to it. During a trip to Rio de Janeiro several years before, I had seen poverty at its worse in the infamous favelas ringing the city. The poor there were a large part of those already ripening for the sharpest danger facing the Western Hemisphere, a Communist take-over. Indeed, there were incongruous facts to consider about the whole of Latin America: industry was growing; the middle class was growing; but poverty was growing faster. In the four decades past, the population had doubled while the average yearly income had been cut in half. The ratio of increased income against population growth was the sorriest in the world—worse even than Africa.

President Kennedy, in a historic effort to cure these ills and counter the threat of political exploitation, had initiated the Alliance For Progress. It was his explicit answer to Teddy Roosevelt's "Speak softly and carry a big stick". He was offering, instead, liberty and free economic development as a way for backward countries to help themselves. To get his program going, he invited all the leaders of the Western Hemisphere to meet with him in Uruguay during the summer. He was making the first major change in American policy toward Latin

America since the Monroe Doctrine. Through the power of his office and the press, the President was setting out to make it an event.

This alone gave the *Crisis Series* an important news-peg. Whatsmore, the series would spell out the real problems of this troubled land that was twice the size of the United States. A project that only a big magazine like *Life* could do well, it was to run over a period of five consecutive weeks. At one heated luncheon, Tim Foote made a last ditch fight to get the editorial board to agree to my shooting the assignment in the Rio favelas. The voting was unanimously against him, and he left the luncheon angered and disappointed.

I was also disappointed. I had never forgotten those ugly slums, festering like sores on the otherwise lovely city of Rio. Ever since my visit there, I had wanted to investigate this tragedy taking place just south of our prosperous land. Tim Foote was a good friend, whom I confided in. He was a short, solidly built young Scotchman with twinkling eyes, and was normally cheerful, but he was a picture of gloom when I met him in his office after his defeat. I expressed my discontent to him with a frank offering of four-letter words.

"It's no use. The powers are against us," he said.

"We shouldn't give up so easily," I answered. Tim sat silently for a few seconds, lightly tapping his pencil against his shell-rim glasses. "Hell, let's keep after them," he suddenly replied. I was encouraged. "It won't be so easy," he added hastily, "but I think we have a strong ally in George Hunt." George was then the assistant managing editor under Ed Thompson.

It wasn't easy. To begin with, poverty was not an appealing subject, especially when the magazine was fighting for survival against television. Certainly a story on rich and exotic Brazil would have been more attractive to its readers. Poverty slopped over into almost all the other categories, and it wasn't particularly entertaining. Everyone on the board wished, I am sure, that poverty, Tim, and I would just go away and leave them in peace.

Nevertheless, Tim and I persisted, and we buttonholed George Hunt and every editor who had an ounce of influence on the project. Everyone I approached seemed sympathetic, but their answers always stemmed from the misconception that I had thoroughly covered poverty for the magazine at some time or other.

"Remember the Red Jackson story you did for us in Harlem?"

"That was about gang warfare, not poverty."

"I remember your doing El Fungito, the Puerto Rican slums."

"But that was over ten years ago."

"My God, has it really been that long?"

"The little boy in rags, the one called *Frog*, is twenty-two years old now."

"Why don't you just go ahead with the board's decision and then see what happens?"

"I know what will happen. *Life* will publish seven different photographs from seven different countries. It's simple." It went on this way for nearly two weeks, until one morning I was handed an amendment to my assignment. Reading it I realized that George Hunt had helped and that Tim and I had won—but there were still certain stipulations. The story would be confined to Rio's favelas, but the Rio news bureau would look for a special type of poor family. I was to select one of my choice; then zero in on the father, show how he supported his family, explore his everyday live, his religion, his politics or social life. Obviously, the story would be a kind of summary, in terms of one individual father, of all the stories in the series. I still wasn't happy. Nor was Tim. It had all the earmarks of a dull and expendable story.

But Tim's wisdom prevailed. "Take it," he advised. "Rio de Janeiro is a long, long way from Rockefeller Plaza. Who knows, you might just misinterpret your instructions. It should be a hell of a lot more interesting and meaningful than the other situation."

Tim Foote was right. It certainly had been more meaningful, I thought, as the plane touched down in New York. As my taxi ground through the heavy city traffic, anxiety overcame me. The undeveloped film in my camera represented the final weeks of shooting; it had seldom been out of my sight. But had my cameras functioned properly? Had the Brazilian heat and humidity affected the film emulsion in some disastrous way? With a shiver I remembered Mario's knocking one camera off the bed to the floor as he ran to escape a thumping from Flavio. But whatever was done was done. The film would be in *Life*'s laboratory before the day was out. After that the worrying would be over.

Tim Foote was smiling as he rose to greet me that same morning of my arrival at the Time-Life Building. "You don't take instructions very well," he quipped. The old familiar twinkle was in his eyes.

"A slight mix-up in communication."

"How's Flavio?"

"Not much hope, I'm afraid.

It was strange to hear Flavio's name spoken so casually here on the other side of the world. By checking all the information that was cabled with each shipment, Tim had got to know the family and their situation as well as anyone in the New York Bureau. His sympathy for them was apparent in the first cable he sent me. We didn't talk much that morning, and I somehow suspected that there still might be some problems surrounding our story, but he assured me that everyone seemed enthusiastic about what they had seen so far.

The film was fine. Two days later I had the enlargements. One glance at Flavio lying ill, his hollow eyes staring at me, jolted me back into his world. Perhaps when *Life en Español*, the Latin American edition, was published, Rio's wealthy might give a little attention to Flavio's side of the mountain. I took the enlargements to the picture editor; then I went home to sleep. It was good to see my own children there, healthy and secure. I slept fitfully that weekend, stirring awake now and then only to sink back into some grim nightmare.

On Monday, when the layout session commenced, my concern about the amount of space Flavio da Silva might get also began. This was the nerve-eroding time when the photographers and reporters sweated it out after a major story was presented to Ed Thompson, the Managing Editor. Now, as many photographers had done many times before, I made a loose estimate: twelve pages of photographs, two for the diary, and a possible cover. Fourteen pages and a cover! Why not? Flavio deserved it.

Time went slowly. Around six o'clock in the evening Tim called. He had the layout in his office. I hurried there but he was across the corridor when I arrived. The layouts were stacked on his desk, and there on top was a full page of Flavio lying in bed. Opposite it was a strikingly beautiful photograph of a woman, shot by Dmitri Kessel. I hastily thumbed through the rest of the pile. There were no other pictures of Flavio.

Tim looked dour when he finally came in.

"Well, that's it, my friend," he said.

I couldn't believe him. "You're kidding," I said.

He shook his head. "No. I'm afraid that's it."

Incredible, but it was so. The two of us stood there in silence. I walked out numbly and made my way up to the layout room. Charlie Tudor, the Art Director, and his assistant were studying some layouts that were tacked to the wall. I walked past them to the table where my diary and the other photographs of Flavio lay. I scooped them up and walked out.

"Where are you going with those?" Charlie asked.

"Home." I must have spoken in a whisper. He repeated his question and I repeated my answer. I went back to my office and remained there in total darkness for several hours, trying to boil out my anger. When I left the building that night I had made up my mind. I would resign.

Ed Thompson was a good editor, and his decisions were usually final. He was tough as nails, gruff and uncommunicative, but there was, I felt, a reluctant gentleness beneath his exterior that made his saltier moods more tolerable. You never expected to make him reverse a decision, but you could gather courage, charge his lair, and try. He would sit quietly impatient, his cold blue eyes challenging you, puffing slowly on a fat cigar as you made your point. Then, after a terrible silence, he could cheer you with a flat "Okay" or chill you with an even flatter "No."

My encounters with Ed had averaged out favorably, but by now anger and disillusionment had pushed me beyond reason. The next morning I got all the way to his door, then turned away, knowing that I was incapable of the patience and clearheadedness needed to save Flavio's story. So I went back to finish working on my resignation, writing finally:

Dear Ed:

I saw the favela layout and I am shocked. I gave so much to it, perhaps too much. I can only remember it now as an exercise in frustration. To use only one picture of this dying boy juxtaposed with that of some socialite is, to my thinking, a journalistic travesty. You will perhaps think I am out of my senses. At this point I probably am. Nevertheless I don't feel that I can work here any longer. With regret I offer my resignation.

I signed the letter and sealed it, with the intention of posting it later. I had loved working for *Life*. It had been extremely good to me. People cared for one another there. It was like working inside a huge family that was scattered to the ends of the earth. Things were not perfect there, but few corporations, if any, could match the concern it showed for its photographers, reporters, and writers. In the furthermost outposts of civilization, in any sort of disaster, you knew that the closest bureau was looking out for you. Once when I became ill in Portugal, a specialist was flown from Paris to attend me. If my family had an emergency while I was away, the New York Bureau took care of it. It was an exciting place to work, and it constantly imbued me with a sense of limitless possibility—to be dispatched to some wonderful place, to do some extraordinary thing. There was no better showcase for a photographer's work than those big, beautifully printed pages which were seen by millions of people every week.

I had spent twelve enjoyable years at *Life*, during which I had acquired a number of good friends. When I was hired in 1948 as the first black photographer on the staff, it was understood that I would not be singled out for any particular assignment because of my color. The editors had been scrupulous about giving me every kind of story, from a gang war to a wedding of European royalty. Up to that time it had been a moveable feast. Now the feast was over.

After a lunch of dry martinis I went back to my office to clean out my desk and pack my photographic equipment. Tim Foote called about three o'clock. Urgency was in his voice. "Have you seen today's *New York Times?*" he asked.

"Nope. What's up?"

"Come up and I'll show you."

Tim had just clipped an article from the *Times* when I entered his office. Smiling, he handed it to me. "Read this," he said. "It could make the difference."

A photograph of Dean Rusk accompanied the article. Reading the meaning in the Secretary of State's words, I began to understand Tim Foote's mood. In effect, Rusk was warning that if our government didn't give immediate and sizable aid to the poor of Latin America, Communism would surely spread rapidly throughout that hemisphere.

"This could make the difference," Tim repeated. He took the article back and hurried down the hall to Ed Thompson's office. I wasn't that encouraged, but since Tim brimmed with such fresh hope, I decided to hold off delivering my resignation for a day or so.

Dean Rusk's words certainly helped make the difference. Late that same afternoon Flavio's full story was scheduled for Part Two of the Latin American series. It didn't get the fourteen pages and the cover I had hoped for. It got eight, with the diary printed on the last two pages of the story. But we were in. I tore up the resignation letter, then sat down and typed a praiseful note to Dean Rusk.

Flavio da Silva's story was published in the issue of June 16, 1961, under the title "Freedom's Fearful Foe: Poverty." No one at the magazine, including me, was totally prepared for what happened next. Within four days after the issue was distributed, letters, many of them including money, began pouring into the Letters Department and to me by the hundreds. At the end of the week they were being relayed to me in bundles and eventually filled several large cartons. The Letters staff worked at top speed, answering mail from all over America. Several of them contained offers to adopt Flavio. For a while I attempted to answer some of the more personal ones myself, but the relentless inflow of letters simply overwhelmed me. I gave up and decided that I would make up several form letters structured to fit the general types of questions being asked. Dozens of these were typed up and I spent several hours signing them. It was exhausting, but it was a joyful kind of exhaustion.

A note came from C. D. Jackson's office, written by Ruth Fowler, an assistant to the publisher of *Life:*

> In eleven years working for *Life* I have never seen any reaction from readers quite as spontaneous as this one . . . we have already set up a Flavio Fund. Queries are coming in from bureaus asking where people may direct money, food, and clothing.

The tremendous response to the story left me in a state of euphoria. But the steep hills of Catacumba, along with the emotional drain of the experience caught up with me unexpectedly one morning. I felt an icy chill, after which I passed out for about ten minutes. Later that afternoon the company doctor ordered me to go somewhere warm for a rest. I took a plane for California the next morning.

My first day in Beverly Hills was less than restful. I gave at least six interviews to the press, radio, and television about Flavio. The entire world seemed to have fallen in love with him. Back in New York the mail and contributions still flooded in. Normally, after several days, letters about a story begin to fall off. Flavio's had escalated. The money sent in was mounting into thousands of dollars. C. D. Jackson cabled George de Carvalho, chief of the Rio de Janeiro Bureau: "We hope to do something for the entire favela as well as Flavio's family—please advise soonest."

While that message was enroute, Barron Beshoar, Denver's bureau head, called with the day's most exciting news. The Children's Asthma Research Institute and Hospital, located in Denver, had volunteered to accept Flavio for two years of treatment, without charge. "We will definitely save him. All you have to do is deliver him to our door," they had told Beshoar. The Institute, already filled to overflowing with more than 150 children, would take Flavio in on an emergency basis. Beshoar was hurriedly instructed to check out the Institute, and its offer.

George de Carvalho's return cable from the Rio bureau advised that there was no way to administer a milk fund, or any such thing, to the entire favela. There were just too many people, more than 25,000, needing thousands of things. "It would be best," he said, "to concentrate on Flavio and his family until something else could be worked out." The next morning Barron Beshoar wired:

THE INSTITUTE'S OFFER STANDS EXACTLY AND PRE-CISELY AS THEY PROMISED. IT IS A REMARKABLE PLACE. THEY HAVE MADE ROOM FOR FLAVIO AL-READY AND FEEL THEIR INSTITUTE IS EXACTLY RIGHT FOR HIM. FROM HIS PHOTOGRAPHS, WHICH REVEAL HIS EXPANDED CHEST AREA, THEY ARE CER-TAIN HE HAS A SEVERE TYPE OF INTRACTABLE ASTHMA.

Ed Thompson conferred with C. D. Jackson, Life's publisher. They talked about my going back to Rio de Janeiro to do a sequel and to bring Flavio to America. Their decision to go ahead with this was relayed to me via long distance telephone by Tim Foote, at seven o'clock in the morning. By noon I was on a plane bound for New York. My convalescence had lasted forty-eight hours and thirty-two minutes.

Preparations for my departure moved at a feverish pitch. The whole of Time Incorporated seemed to be at my disposal. Tickets, releases for Flavio's parents to sign, medical forms, passports, legal documents, expense money, film, medicine, and other necessities were hastily assembled. To convince those who just couldn't believe that such poverty existed, I bought a thirty-five-millimeter motion picture camera, hoping to record the conditions there.

A disturbing wire came from the Rio bureau that urged us on:

FLAVIO HAS TAKEN A TURN FOR THE WORSE. DOCTOR FIRMINO GOMES RIBEIRO THINKS FLAVIO IS PROBABLY A TUBERCULAR VICTIM. UNCERTAIN WHETHER ASTHMA'S ORIGIN IS ALLERGY OR CONGENITAL. IT'S AN APPALLING, CRIPPLING STRAIN. DURING ASTHMATIC CRISIS HIS NORMALLY SALLOW SKIN TURNS FAINT-BLUE, VEINS THROB, AND THROAT SWELLS IN EFFORT TO BREATHE. IN LAST SEVERAL DAYS HE SUFFERED THREE BAD SPELLS. IN EACH HE BEGAN DOING THE FAMILY'S WORK BEFORE OVERCOMING CRISIS. CURRENTLY HE'S ILL AND FEVERISH WITH FLU, BUT HAS NOT TAKEN ANY MEDICINE OR TREATMENT OF ANY KIND. HE'S STILL KILLING HIMSELF TO KEEP FAMILY GOING. PRIME NEED IS TO HOSPITALIZE HIM AS SOON AS POSSIBLE TO PREVENT EARLY DEATH. LIFE'S READERS WHO SENT CONTRIBUTIONS CAN PROBABLY SAVE HIS LIFE. WE HAVE TO HURRY.

A couple of things disturbed me about this cable. If Flavio was tubercular, there were U.S. health laws to prevent his entering this country. President Kennedy was the only one who could waive the law in Flavio's case. "Don't worry. If it becomes necessary the President will be alerted," I was told. The other problem, I felt, was our obligation to move the Da Silvas out of the favela before the July issue of *Life en Español* was published in Latin America. Their life on Catacumba would be impossible after that. Everyone agreed. José Gallo was asked to look for a suitable house for them, miles from the favela.

It was incredible. Little more than a week had gone by since the story's publication, and I was returning to a boy I had never expected to see again.

Four

On the plane back to Brazil I remembered how I used to lie awake as a child and wish for things I felt I would never have. Flavio seldom expressed a desire for much of anything. He hadn't been exposed to much. Simple things such as cutlery, bed linen, shoes, or a radio, even a curtained window, had been denied him. Now things would be different.

José Gallo was at the airport to meet me the next morning. We embraced. "Well, Gordon my friend, miracles do happen," he said.

"How's Flavio?" I asked.

"Somewhat better today. He's excited. He knows you're coming."

As we drove toward the city he explained his plans for moving the Da Silvas out of the favela. A house had been found for them in the Guadalupe District several miles outside Rio. "It

even has a cottage in the backyard," José said. "They can rent it
out for extra income. *Life* has agreed to advance the money for
the purchase." My heart warmed again to this organization. It
was doing a good and thorough job. José went on to say that a
small van had been rented to move the family. There was so
little for them to move. Perhaps they would give their shack to
neighbors.

"You are of course planning to return to Denver with us," I
said.

José's eyes shifted lazily toward me. "Really?" he asked,
somehow not believing.

"Of course. We will need an interpreter," I answered.

It would be his first trip to the United States. And it was evi-
dent, even in his impassive features, that he was slowly filling
with excitement. I had grown to admire this quiet, slow-eyed,
slow-talking man. I knew he was constantly pained by his own
handicapped son, Carlos. The eight-year-old boy had a brain
injury which rendered him incapable of speech. Yet José's attention and love for Flavio never lagged, and he shared his
pain for his own son with his pain for Flavio.

I arose early the next morning and left word at my hotel for
José to meet me up at the Da Silva place. The taxi left me at the
bottom of the hill across the street from the entrance to the
favela. I stood for a moment looking up at the mountainside,
finding it hard to believe I was back. There it was, horrible,
hot, and as smelly as ever. As I started to move off, a child's
voice called from the crowd of favelados milling about the entrance. "Gorduun! Gorduun!" It was little Batista, the dark,
calm Da Silva child. He smiled as he darted across the street to
meet me. "Wait, Batista!" I shouted. It was too late.

There was a screech of car brakes. In the next instant the car
knocked him down, passed over him, stopped, then started off
again. But by now a dozen or more favelados surrounded the

car, screaming threats at the driver. I rushed to Batista's prostrate form. He was breathing and bore no external wounds, but his eyes rolled eerily in their sockets. He appeared unconscious. I lifted him from the pavement. The crowd grew quickly, and became violent, rocking the car back and forth while two men tried to force open the locked doors. The frightened driver could only sit there helplessly. Next I heard the hysterical but familiar voice of Nair da Silva. "My God! My God! They have killed my boy," she screamed, pushing her way through the crowd.

With Batista in one arm I began beating on the car door. "Hospital! Hospital!" I shouted. The driver unlocked the rear door. I pushed Nair into the car, laid Batista in her arms, got in myself, and motioned for the driver to pull away. The hostile crowd slowly drew back and we started off. As we sped along the driver kept babbling apologies, but Nair ignored him as she rocked back and forth in her grief. I tried to comfort her, but she was not to be consoled. The happy reunion I had hoped for had turned into tragedy.

At the hospital we waited as the doctors examined Batista behind closed doors. The nurse offered Nair a seat but she refused it. She stood, wringing her hands, weeping, and mumbling prayers for her son. Before long José da Silva arrived with José Gallo. The father was barefoot with his pants rolled up to his knees. His shirt hung loose and unbuttoned, and he held a battered hat in his hand.

"How is the boy, Nair?" he asked gruffly.

"He is in God's hands," she answered softly.

José da Silva bent his head and prayed, for this was his favorite child. In fact, the four of us stood there praying. Then we heard Batista crying. At least he was alive. But nearly an hour passed before the doctor came to give his report. "Your child has a badly fractured collarbone," he said to the mother. "So far we can't find any internal injuries. There are no serious head injuries. He is lucky, just stunned by the jolt. Don't worry, he will be all right." Then the doctor disappeared. I suddenly remembered the driver whom I had last seen at the end of the corridor. I turned to look for him. He was gone and so was his car.

When they brought Batista out some time later, his shoulder was in a cast and his right arm in a sling. He was bright-eyed now and unafraid. His father carried him to José Gallo's car and we returned to the favela. Once inside the shack Batista's gleaming white bandages seemed somehow incongruous in the soiled atmosphere. The other brothers and sisters seemed more curious than concerned about Batista's accident. For a moment or so he was something of a hero to the others, but soon all their excitement was turned upon the news that Flavio would be going to a hospital in America and that they were going to have a new home far away from the favela. José Gallo told them with a sort of restrained joy. He ended by saying gently, "Not only will you have a new home but also new furniture, good food, and new clothes to wear."

The children went into hysterics. They couldn't contain themselves. They jumped about laughing, dancing, and playfully shoving one another. Flavio was equally happy but his last attack had left him weak. He just sat quietly on the floor with a broad smile on his face. Nair accepted the word in stunned silence as she slumped on the bed with Zacarias in her arms. José da Silva reacted strangely, his eyes holding us between his awe and disbelief. It seemed as if he thought we were involving him in some sort of trickery. Flavio at last got to his feet and shook my hand. "I'm glad you came back," he said. His voice had a calm and warmth that left me speechless. I could only think of his wish for "a real house with pots and pans, and a bed with sheets," and that, miraculously, it was coming true.

José and I had stayed on for the remainder of the afternoon, filling Flavio's parents in on the events back in America that

were so drastically changing their lives. Nair showed some concern about Flavio's having to be gone for two years, but she
easily accepted its necessity. The main thing she wanted was
for her son to live. José, the father, was more concerned about
moving away from the favela. "You can forget the favela," José
Gallo assured him. "You'll have a far better life and a chance to
earn a living where you are going. Don't worry about it now."
But the suspicious man, unconvinced that he wasn't a victim of
some queer game, sat scratching his head in puzzlement.

It was eight o'clock at night when José and I left and started
down the hill. We were quiet, talked out, but happy, and with
good reason. This day, which had begun so disastrously, had
ended cheerfully.

The Rio bureau had been meticulous in its search for a new
home for the Da Silvas. José Gallo had put particular emphasis
on selecting a neighborhood where the pressure of economic
and social problems would not overwhelm them. He had
looked at more than twenty houses in as many locations
throughout the surrounding suburbs. The right bungalow had
finally turned up in a low-cost housing project in the district of
Guadalupe, located about an hour by car from the Catacumba
favela. The area was clean, orderly, and spacious. It had all the
basic utilities that most Americans take for granted: streets,
sidewalks, sewers, tapwater, electricity, schools, health facilities, and police protection.

The house itself had a front and back porch, a planted front
garden, and a back yard that had been cemented for cleanliness. It was shaded by a lovely tropical tree. There were two
small bedrooms, a living room, an alcove, a kitchen, and a
bathroom with a tub and shower. Compared to the favela, the
neighborhood was a paradise, and next to their shack, the bungalow was a palace. The price for it was 750,000 cruzeiros—just
under $3,000. By American standards it was worth about

$7,500. There was an important extra—a small cottage in back with two rooms, kitchen, and bathroom. If the family did not choose to use it, it could be rented out for steady income.

The sale had been closed on the Saturday before. Flavio, José Gallo, and I were already booked to fly to the States on the following Wednesday. Flavio would spend one day in the house with his family. In this way he would not have only the favela nightmare to remember.

But the house was in bad shape. It had needed painting inside and out. Electrical wiring dangled loose and the cement was cracked. There was no stove or furniture. Word was spread. A dozen neighborhood workmen took over. In one weekend, without charge, they did a week's worth of labor. Their pay was simply satisfaction, beer, and black beans and rice. *Life* had supplied the materials with which the men did the painting, sanding, and patching. The place now looked like new. The self-appointed foreman of the crew expressed everyone's feeling. "Lots of us came here from the favelas. We want them to start out right. We're glad to help."

On Monday Sears Roebuck delivered all the furniture that was needed. The neighbors came again and installed everything—a dinette and two bedroom sets, living room divans, tables and chairs, and a gas stove. There was also tableware, linen and towels, plenty of soap, toothpaste, and twenty toothbrushes. It was all there waiting.

Early Monday morning I arrived at the shack to take Flavio downtown for some new clothes. He seemed better now. I watched as he washed himself in the same pan in which he had for so long cooked the rice and beans. He then began pulling out his belongings from the drawer where Nair kept the laundered things. The best he could find was a ragged shirt and a pair of tattered pants. He put them on and we went down the hill. Both of us tried, without success, to keep our calm, but our excitement showed all over us. The fact that he was barefoot bothered me, but since Flavio had never owned a pair of shoes, he hadn't seemed to give it a thought.

We took a taxi to Rio's business section, got out, and looked for a boy's clothing store. We found one after pushing our way through the crowds along the main thoroughfare. An awkward moment arose when we entered the store. The clerks stood looking at the ragged boy with contempt. Flavio didn't notice them; he was too busy looking at the glass cases of shoes in the center of the room. With calculated ease I pulled a large wad of cruzeiros from one pocket and put it into another one. The clerks moved in on us with the warmest courtesy, and after an hour in the store Flavio walked out looking like a student from Eton. But now that he was dressed like other boys he looked more sickly than ever. He would need a lot of good meals to properly fill the new suit he was wearing.

This was his first suit, his first pair of shoes. He hobbled along in them, smiling, making an effort to look as though he had worn them all his life. As he walked his socks kept slipping down. There wasn't enough flesh on his legs to hold them up. But Flavio glowed with happiness. We went back to my hotel, and there he took his first real bath in a tub. For this special occasion I bought some bubble bath and added a generous portion of it to the hot water. I scrubbed him from head to foot for at least twenty minutes, then left him to soak. He enjoyed it immensely and asked for another sudsing. It was just as well that he did; the water was black. The first attempt had only loosened the surface dirt. It finally took three tubs of hot water, and a lot more scrubbing to get through the twelve years of dirt ingrained in his skin.

Toweled and sweet-smelling, he dressed again, then went to the balcony outside my room. There he stood for some time gazing down on the patterned sidewalks running alongside the elegant waterfront. he had seen it only once before, when I had taken him and Mario on their first trip to the beach.

Flavio asked to have dinner out there, so before going to shower I ordered steak, vegetables, salad, milk, and custard. When the food arrived later, Flavio seemed to observe it with awe. The uniformed waiter, the white tablecloth and folded napkins, the crested dishware and sparkling silver were things he had never encountered before. It puzzled me that now the food was in front of him he made no attempt to eat it.

"Eat, Flavio. It's for you," I said.

He shook his head slowly, waving off my invitation with his hand. He then got up and went into the bedroom and closed the door leading to the patio. Something was bothering him. Through the lace curtains I could see that he was taking something from his pocket and placing it on the bed. He returned, smiling now, and began to eat with gusto.

A while later I figured out what had been bothering him. I had left a pile of cruzeiros on the bed; while I was showering he had pocketed some of them. It was understandable. He hadn't seen that much money in his entire lifetime. It was careless of me to have left it there so openly. But it was comforting to know that his conscience had gotten the better of him. I congratulated him for his honesty and explained that he would never have to steal again. Embarrassed, he shook his head, seeming to understand.

It was natural that the Da Silva children would spread the news that they had been asked to keep quiet. Immediately they shouted it to the hills. In doing so, they incurred the wrath of a number of other favelados, and Nair was forced to carry a broomstick to ward off the attacks against Maria, Luzia, and Mario. But hostility could be expected from those who would have to remain on Catacumba. "Why them and not us?" they asked. It was a good question.

When José and I arrived with the moving van early the next morning, the entire family was washing up with their last bucket of water. Flavio was hobbling about wrapping their few belongings in bundles. Some of the friendlier neighbors stood just outside the shack looking on with obvious sorrow. They had shared the misery of this hill with José and Nair for more than twelve years. Some confessed that they were glad to see them go. One woman, a godparent to Luzia, said, "Maybe little Flavio will live now."

Very soon we were ready to start down the hill. Everything they owned could be carried in makeshift knapsacks. As they left, Nair held back for one last look around the grubby place that had been home to her for so long. Some of the neighbors followed us all the way to the bottom, where a hundred or more people had gathered at the entrance. As the family moved past the other favelados, the mood was tense and solemn. A few good-byes came from the crowd. One woman came forward and kissed Zacarias, then Nair, and turned back up the hill in tears. Another woman standing by with a small child in her arms grabbed my shoulder.

"What about us? All the rest of us stay here to die!" she demanded. I looked at her for a moment, answerless, then moved away. We piled into the van and as it pulled out Flavio strained for a look at the hill.

"Look! Look!" he said. "There it is!" He was pointing far up to their deserted shack. "Good-bye, favela," Mario said. He was smiling. I glanced back. The crowd was still there, watching our departure from a lengthening distance. "This is a very happy day," Flavio said. "It's the happiest day of our lives."

Five

We stopped first at Sears Roebuck to buy the entire family new clothes. Entering the store the kids were startled by the popping flashbulbs; a score of newsmen went after them like hawks after chickens. Bedlam followed, with the children out of control, grabbing dolls and toys they had never dreamed of owning. Sales clerks fluttered about helplessly while the newsmen, their cameras flashing, grabbed at the children, posing them in incongruous situations. Little Zacarias was photographed with a teddy bear on his lap that was three times his size. Mario was asked to slop about in men's cowboy boots. Petite Albia was hoisted atop a big motorbike, where she hung on in absolute fright, and Luzia was squeezed into an oversized doll house. Sanity returned only after José Gallo corralled the family into one corner of the store and barred the newsmen.

In the end, José da Silva chose for himself a cheap blue suit, and Nair selected three smocks, three outfits for Zacarias, and something for the new child coming soon. Each girl got three cotton dresses, underwear, shoes, and stockings. Maria chose a pink dress that was too long, but the salesgirls hitched it up for her and put a hem in it. The boys each got three sets of shirts, pants, sweaters, socks, and shoes. Then everyone got a pair of pajamas to forestall their sleeping in the clothes they wore all week.

Toys were next. The girls instinctively picked dolls, the boys' choices ran to water pistols, cars, trains, footballs and baseballs, bats, and cowboy outfits. All of them insisted on changing their clothes in the store aisles. At the very last minute someone saw that Batista's shoes were two sizes too large. They were quickly exchanged, and everyone marched from the store transformed. All the things that had been denied them on past Christmases were now theirs.

The half hour trip to the Guadalupe district became tumultuous, with the children noisily grabbing at each others' possessions. At one point José da Silva, who was growing more unnerved by the moment, screamed for quiet. It lasted about a minute before disorder broke out again, and we pulled into the block where a good part of the neighborhood had turned out to greet the Da Silvas.

A startling hush fell over the family as they all got out and entered their new home. The Da Silvas went in almost timidly. Going through the gate José da Silva nervously bowed to the neighbors who, one by one, returned their greetings. Once inside the Da Silvas fell completely silent, as if they disbelieved what they were seeing. Finally Nair murmured, "Good Lord, this is all for us?"

"All for you," José Gallo murmured softly.

Flavio then ventured out in front of the group and looked things over. Then in a half-whisper he asked, "Will my family really live here when I am gone?"

"It's their home forever," José answered.

Luzia, who had tried so hard to keep clean in the favela, inched her way into the bathroom. She touched the bidet, climbed onto it and inspected herself in the mirror. "Come! Come!" she called to Maria. Suddenly, like a dam bursting, Maria and the others poured all over the house, pulling out drawers, inspecting the beds, flushing the toilet over and over. Nair moved cautiously into the kitchen and rubbed her hand across the refrigerator, then the stove. The neighborhood women had unpacked and washed every plate, knife, fork, and spoon. They had stocked the cupboards with enough staples for a month. Fresh potato salad was in the refrigerator. *Feijoada*, a rich Brazilian dish of rice, black beans, meat, and vegetables simmered in a large pot on the stove. José went to the kitchen and looked around, then moved to the door and surveyed the little cottage sitting at the edge of the paved back yard.

"I can't believe this," he murmured for the dozenth time.

When at last the Da Silvas sat down to eat, the wives of the same men in the neighborhood who had worked to put the house in shape served them. Everyone had at least three helpings, and for once Flavio did not have to feed everyone. "Oh boy," he said, "this is more than I ever had to eat at home in my whole life."

By eight o'clock the neighbors had cleaned up the kitchen, made up the beds, and gone. For the children the magical day was coming to an end. Mario and Batista giggled at one another as they fumbled with the buttons on their new pajamas. Luzia was drying her doll's face with a towel after washing it in the bidet. Albia and Isabel, the two smallest children, had fallen asleep on the bedroom floor, entwined in a Siamese-twin embrace. When Flavio saw this he lifted each child into her separate bunk bed, undressed her, and covered her with a sheet. This would be his last look at them for at least two years, as our plane was scheduled to take off at midnight.

Maria was the last to get into her nightgown. She stood silently watching Flavio pack the last of his things. Neither she nor Flavio ever said good-bye to one another. They faced each other rather awkwardly. He giggled and pushed her. She giggled and shoved back. Then she ran into the darkness of her room.

Flavio and I drifted out to the backyard where José Gallo and José da Silva were talking. "Are you sure they won't kick us out next week and take all this stuff back?" Da Silva was still suspicious and disbelieving. Again, José Gallo assured him that everything there was his to keep. But he warned, "You can only trade or sell this house for a better one. That is in the contract, José."

Flavio asked, "Can I have a truck?"

"But you already have a fire truck," José replied.

"No," Flavio said, pacing the length of the porch, "a big one *para meu pai* ('for my father') to get work with."

"We'll see, we'll see," José answered.

Nair da Silva, I noticed, avoided Flavio most of the day. Not once in the excitement of those last twelve hours had she spoken to him or touched him. Her withdrawal seemed even more pronounced now as she sat alone in the kitchen, wiping aimlessly at some kitchenware. By ten o'clock her manner had become one of stoical indifference.

When the time to leave arrived, Flavio came up behind her and touched her arm. "I've come to say good-bye, Momma," he said. Nair didn't move. Puzzled, he looked toward me. I motioned him toward her. This time he attempted to put his arm around her. "I'm sorry but I have to go now, Momma."

Suddenly Nair turned and, in a spasm of grief, enclosed him tightly in her arms, sobbing hoarsely. "Go, my son. God protect you."

Confused, Flavio took some coins from his pocket and

pressed them into his mother's hand. Then he hurriedly picked
up his suitcase, took my hand, and pulled me from the house.

Flavio's father was waiting in José Gallo's car for the trip to
the airport. He had decided at the last moment to see his son
off. By now this son was undoubtedly the most celebrated
twelve-year-old in the Western Hemisphere. A battery of
floodlights, newsmen, and television cameras met us as we entered the terminal, and hundreds of people closed in to get a
look at Flavio. At first he appeared to be taking it all in stride;
then suddenly the strain of the day, the past week, pushed him
to the breaking point. He ducked under my arm to hide from
the cameras, and broke into tears. I hurried him through the
crowd to where Varig's airline officials waited, and sensing
Flavio's hysteria, they rushed us straight to the plane.

At the bottom of the ramp I asked José da Silva how he felt
about someone adopting Flavio. He scratched his head, thinking for a moment, then answered, "I don't care how long you
keep him. Just remember he's ours. Bring him back well." He
touched Flavio on the shoulder. "Be a good boy," he said
sternly. Then he moved off to the edge of the airstrip. We
could still see him standing there in the half-darkness as the
jets whined and the big plane moved toward the runway. José
Gallo leaned across the aisle and pointed in his direction. "That
poor guy is still wondering about what happened to him."

Once Flavio was inside the plush first-class cabin, he com-
posed himself and settled into his seat. He tensed as the
motors roared, and we began streaking down the runway. As
we shot up into the night his fingernails dug into the back of my
hand. "Next stop, New York," José said. Flavio lay back and
relaxed into a smile. Minutes after we leveled off the stewardess brought him slipper socks, a vial of cologne, an eye
shield, chocolates, and a model of the plane in which he was
flying. There was dinner again, but Flavio was, for the second

time in his life, too excited to eat. Possibly the most thrilling moment for him came when the pilot took him forward to the cockpit. There he saw "lots of blinking lights and some men in police uniforms driving the plane." Surely he was tired, but only after the dinner hour was over and the cabin lights were dimmed did he give in to sleep. I looked at him, wondering what he was dreaming about. Whatever his dreams, they could not possibly prefigure the life he was about to begin. Nothing in his experience could prepare him for that. It was enough to know that he was heading for something far better than he was leaving.

It was not Flavio's birthday, but evidently Varig Airlines wanted to create one for him. The next morning, about two hours away from New York, the stewardess carried in a large cake resplendent with candles and heaped with frosting. The pilot came back and at his signal everyone began singing in Portuguese, "Happy birthday, dear Flavio, happy birthday to you." Flavio blushed deeply, and with a little urging, he got up and blew out the candles with one puff. All the passengers clapped and cheered, and Flavio smiled broadly and waved everyone up for a sliver of his cake. It was a good moment.

The final results of Flavio's X-rays had ruled out tuberculosis, so we went through the health and immigration department without any problems. The official who inspected our passports recognized Flavio from his pictures in *Life* and wished him a pleasant stay in America. As usual, Flavio seemed startled to discover that complete strangers knew his name, especially so far away from the favela. Vivi Stiles, an assistant to Ruth Fowler in the publisher's office, and a registered nurse awaited us in a chauffeured limousine. In minutes we were headed for New York's Dorset Hotel, where a suite of rooms had been reserved. Flavio would be taken to a doctor for a preliminary examination, after which he would rest over night. We would continue to Denver the following morning. I had planned to take Flavio home for a day in the country, but the doctor advised against this; so I left him with José at the hotel. There was disappointment in my household when I arrived in White Plains without him, for my children had looked forward to him as they would a new brother. I pacified them somewhat by giving them a detailed account of everything that had happened on my return to Rio.

José Gallo telephoned me about nine o'clock that evening with disturbing news. Flavio had gone to bed and awakened, feeling ill. He had gone to the bathroom, vomited, and had fainted on the way back to his room. José had discovered him as he lay moaning in the hallway. It had never occurred to Flavio to call for help; in the favela he usually handled his attacks by himself. There was another problem: Flavio had refused to remove his shoes—even in bed. He was afraid someone might steal them. Before hanging up, I asked José if he thought we would be able to leave for Denver on schedule. "It looks doubtful," he replied. Flavio slept well the rest of the night beside a huge stuffed dog the doctor had given him. He was bright and cheerful the next morning, and after the doctor had examined him we were given permission to travel.

As we landed at Denver, I could see an ambulance and a sizable crowd waiting. Flavio got off the plane smiling, but halfway down the ramp the flashbulbs started popping, and once again he ducked beneath my arm. But the Institute kept the reception under control, and the fussing over him to a minimum. Once Flavio arrived at the Institute, they allowed a few photographs to be taken of their celebrated new patient on the playground with some of the other children. Then everything was halted so that he could have an hour's rest before the doctors examined him. José and I sighed with relief; Flavio was at last in the hands of people who could save him.

Flavio officially entered the Children's Asthma Research Institute and Hospital (CARIH) on July 7, 1961. Dr. Samuel

Bukantz, the Institute's medical and research director, Dr. Constantine J. Falliers, and Dr. Marcello Behar conducted Flavio's first examination three hours after his arrival in Denver. Flavio seemed bewildered and a little startled when the three men entered the examination room, despite their gentle manner. He sat nervously on a sheet-covered table picking at his fingernails. Dr. Falliers, who was to head the medical team directly concerned with Flavio's treatment, asked us to undress him for X-rays, but Flavio refused to remove his clothes. Someone suggested that he might cooperate if I undressed, too. This worked—until we got to his shoes. After he absolutely refused to take them off we decided to use force. José and I held him down while the doctors pulled off one shoe. Flavio shrieked with such pain that they examined the foot before attempting to remove the other shoe. It was covered with sores and blisters. We decided to cut the other shoe off. His tears cascaded when he saw his beautiful shoe cut to pieces, and promises that he would get another pair just like them didn't help. After Flavio had cried himself out, the doctors went on with their work. A couple of hours later, in a new pair of sneakers, Flavio was pumping wildly on a playground swing, surrounded by admiring boys and girls. It seemed that he wouldn't be in need of friends.

"To help a child to health is to walk with God" was the motto for the "Home," as the children called the Institute. It sat on seventeen sprawling acres in north Denver. Walking around the campus that afternoon, I saw playgrounds with the young patients pumping in swings, riding seesaws, slides, and carousels, and playing volleyball and baseball. Looking at them it was hard to realize they were ill. Some looked dwarfed, which is a characteristic deformity of young asthmatics, and some who were under heavy cortisone treatment had a fat-faced look, but the general atmosphere was one of healthy children having a good time. I continued through the hospital, research laboratories, the community cafeteria, and one of the five dormitories and decided that Flavio had landed at the right place. Indeed, it was a far cry from the mountain-side of Catacumba. The Institute, I was told, had been treating asthmatic children for nearly seventy years. Its live-in program was started back in 1939 when it was found that moving a child from its home environment often brought improvement—and with little need of medication. Squabbling parents, it was discovered, could bring on attacks as well as animal fur, plant life, or some particular kind of food. Just isolating a child from everyday emotional situations and family problems made it easier to track down that child's allergy.

The Institute accommodated 150 children from six to sixteen. There was a staff of three senior doctors, five psychologists, five allergy trainees, two dieticians, and ten house parents. It took a lot of money to run the place; the cost of care for one child amounted to well over $10,000 a year. Treatment, nevertheless, was free. The Institute was funded by philanthropic organizations, private endowments, and Federal agencies.

Everything was done to keep the children's lives as normal as possible. The sickest ones were hospitalized, and all the others were sent to Denver public schools. They were bussed to church on Sundays, to the movies and other amusement places on the weekends. In case of a sudden asthmatic attack, they were trained to help themselves until they could get to a hospital for treatment.

Flavio would no longer have to survive on stale coffee, hard rice, and black beans. His meals would be prepared under the supervision of trained dieticians and consulting allergists. Dr. Falliers and his team were, I knew, dedicated to saving Flavio's life; nonetheless he was in a strange place with only a few words to express his needs or his feelings. Surely he would feel isolated and fearful for awhile. It was disturbing just to think of all the adjustments he would have to make. In the months ahead the staff would have to try and undo what twelve years of poverty and hardship had done.

I hoped that all of his ills and the lack of nutrition had not already permanently damaged him mentally and physically, as it had done to so many favela children; for even now he had started to withdraw into his own dark world, more and more unmindful of his condition and demanding less for himself. The emotional problems developing inside him could affect his later life, if indeed he had a later life. There had been times on Catacumba when I felt that he was getting ready to die, that perhaps something inside his overtaxed body had decided that it could endure no more, that it was giving up. If this was so, I hoped there was still time to save him. Before leaving that afternoon, I spent an hour alone with Flavio and José. I told Flavio that the doctors who cut up his shoe did so to keep from hurting him. "Those are good men who will make you well." He nodded his head as if he understood.

We had sandwiches and tea, walked about the campus for a little while; then it was time for me to go. Flavio walked to the entrance where my taxi was waiting; we embraced and I left for my plane to New York. José would stay on for two weeks to interpret, as well as quell the uneasiness Flavio would surely experience.

As my plane climbed through the clouds I looked out the window, trying to spot the Institute. The city was already gone from sight, but there, riding the gray clouds below, was the shadow of the plane, the "pilot's cross." To the pilots of the fighter group I had once flown with as a correspondent, this was a sign of good luck. For Flavio's sake I hoped they were right.

Before settling in for a nap I took from my jacket pocket a scribbled note from Dr. Falliers. It read: "Flavio's enlarged chest cavity confirms suspicion that he has one of the severest types of asthma. And X-ray indicates that at twelve he has the bone structure of a boy nine. His weight and height are those of a six-year-old." I looked out again for the pilot's cross. It was gone.

Six

Flavio's story had been published on June 16, 1961. On July 21, thirty-odd days later, *Life*'s cover portrayed Flavio smiling his thanks to those thousands who had helped him. Inside, twelve pages of photographs showed readers the good they had done for Flavio and his family. But those pages made it clear that in molding human lives, money could not finish what it had begun. The Da Silvas would have to build on their own miracle, not lapse into dependency. Furthermore, a smiling Flavio did not solve the problems he dramatized. He was just one of a numberless multitude, a symbol, a medium through which one could understand the tragedy of poverty. Perhaps his story could inspire the massive help required to give some measure of well-being to all those who so desperately needed it.

The response to Flavio's story was still overwhelming. The

number of letters and contributions was by now far greater than anything we ever expected. Nearly $30,000 in silver, bills, and checks had come in. My office alone held four large cartons of letters, and I spent a week answering only those that asked for information the Letters Department couldn't supply. Flavio's fund was swelling fast; Ruth Fowler was trying to find some practical way to disburse it. It was decided that the contributors themselves might help determine how the money should be divided. There were far too many of them to be contacted personally; so a request for their advice was published in *Life*. The opinions were almost unanimously in favor of the fund being shared equally by Flavio, his family, and the Catacumba favela. With President Kennedy's Alliance for Progress as a model, Catacumba could now become a pilot *project for progress*. This plan was immediately accepted by the publisher's office and Ruth Fowler, with the help of José Gallo, would oversee all three of the funds.

But every tree branch harbors a few angry crows. None seemed angrier than the Brazilian magazine *O Cruzeiro*. After Flavio's story was published in *Life en Español*, *O Cruzeiro* rushed one of its own photographers to New York City to do a similar story on a Puerto Rican family in the Wall Street district, and it depicted a sleeping child with cockroaches crawling over its face, and another child crying from hunger. It accused *Life* of fabricating the whole favela story, and accused me of buying a coffin and planting a live woman in it. (Actually the woman was indeed dead, with mortuary records to prove it, and she was not in a coffin but lying on a makeshift bier.) *Time Magazine* discovered, after an investigation, that *O Cruzeiro's* correspondent had posed the picture of the sleeping child, having caught the roaches and pasted them on the child's face. To get the other child to cry, the photographer had threatened to shove it out the window. The wonder of it all was why *O Cruzeiro* had felt it necessary to go to such lengths. If it had gone to New York's Harlem, or Chicago's South Side, they could have found a story as genuinely tragic as the one of Catacumba. When *Time* published its findings, *O Cruzeiro* fell quiet.

A few minor protests rose from other Brazilian publications as well. Rio de Janeiro's journal *O Dia* commented:

> "It is not necessary for foreigners to tell us that our slums are monstrosities. We know this better than they do. We wish to do away with this shameful situation. If the government fails to do it we will do it ourselves. The fault is not that of the people. But without a doubt *Life* gave us an eye-opener. We should remember the famous decree of Capistrano de Abreu, in which the historian declared the necessity of having shame. The day will come in which we will have it in abundance, so that more reports (like *Life*'s) will not come from the outside."

Rio's *Corredo da Manha* wrote:

> The misery of our slum family was shown to the world. In return this family received a decent house. The photographs showed various children and some of the adult neighbors of the Da Silva family. These neighbors will be waiting for some United States magazine to make a report that will get them clean houses. We do not expect our own authorities will answer them. We are not making suggestions. The photographs in *Life* speak for themselves. And they speak loudly.

This was the general tone of the Brazilian press, who as a whole praised *Life*'s coverage, while openly admitting that it was something they should have done themselves.

e Catacumba Favela, Rio de Janeiro, 1961. The Da Silva shack is near the top, just beneath
e Christ figure (Cristo Redentor). (*Gorden Parks*)

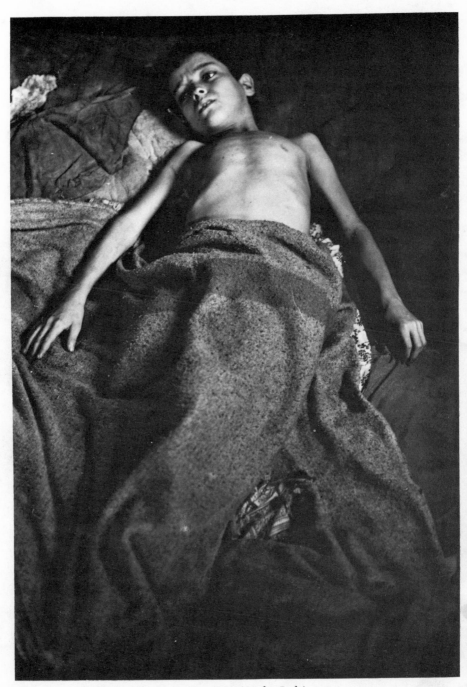

Flavio da Silva during an asthmatic seizure, 1961. (*Gordon Parks*)

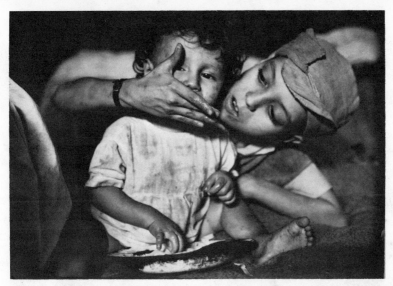

Flavio feeds Zacarias. (*Gordon Parks*)

lavio prepares supper for the family.
ordon Parks)

A deceased neighbor of the Da Silva family,
Catacumba favela, 1961. (*Gordon Parks*)

Early morning, the Da Silva Shack. Flavio arises first to begin the daily chores. (*Gordon Parks*)

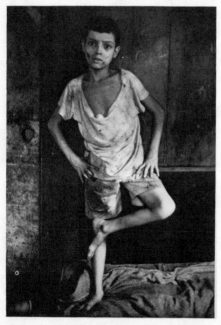

Flavio da Silva, the favela, 1961. (*Gordon Parks*)

Flavio gets his first suit and new shoes, 1961. (*Gordon Parks*)

The Da Silva's new home in the Guadalupe District, outside Rio de Janeiro, 1961. (*Gordon Parks*)

...avio being examined by the clinic
...ctors in Denver, Colorado, 1961.
...*ordon Parks*)

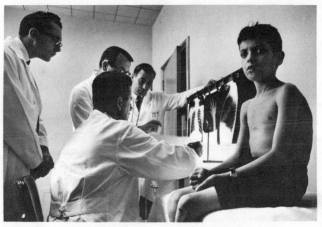

Jose da Silva with Nair, holding Zacarias, and his sister-in-law. They stand at the window of their new home. (*Gordon Parks*)

Flavio's second day at the Asthma Research Institute, 1961. (*Gordon Parks*)

Flavio with Gordon Parks at the Rio airport, 1961. (*Gordon Parks*)

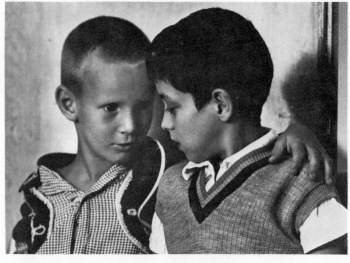

my Ebbe and Flavio
e friends at the Institute,
. (*Gordon Parks*)

Flavio's second day at the Asthma Research Institute, 1961. (*Gordon Parks*)

Jimmy Gaddy and Flavio at the Institute, 1961. (*Gordon Parks*)

Seven

Flavio is a puzzle to us. We, as a team of medical men, psychiatrists, psychologists, and teachers, are trying to solve the enigma he presents. He is constantly going back to catch up with himself. He is participating in things that he missed when he was much younger, say five, six, seven, or eight years old. It is just the opposite of what the normal child does who progresses to more mature pursuits. He is always trying to start from where he should have started in the first place. We try now to formulate a strategy to cope with him. There is the abrupt shock of his leaving Rio's poverty situation and the other shock of coming to this country under such abnormal conditions. There is the general environmental problem. He is so awfully serious, much more so than kids twice his age. This is because he shouldered a certain kind of responsibility back in the favela—his brothers and sisters and their day-to-day problems. This seriousness also puzzles us. We ourselves are learning an awful lot in trying to break through the barrier of his behavior patterns.

From a report in Flavio da Silva's medical file, 1961, by Dr. Constantine John Falliers

There was an enormous difference between Flavio's case and those of the other patients at the Institute. Although he underwent the same kind of attacks they suffered, he carried the extra burden of malnutrition. He weighed only forty-six-and-a-half pounds, and stood a bare inch and a half over four feet. His teeth were in terrible condition. His feet were badly infected. His hearing was impaired because of massive accumulations of wax in his ears. There was the language barrier, cultural shock, and, as far as the doctors were concerned, he was still a candidate for tuberculosis. For these reasons he was not immediately assigned to a dormitory, but placed in a hospital room for the first week, where four times daily his feet were soaked in warm water and he was given antibiotics.

The hospital room was cheerful, with a comfortable bed, a chair, reading lamp, radio, and a desk supplied with picture books, crayons, and drawing paper. From his window Flavio could look out to the green lawns and playgrounds. He was placed under close observation, but he was not confined to his bed; whenever possible he was encouraged to mix and play with the other children. He was examined more frequently than other incoming patients, sometimes three or four times within twenty-four hours. Often, when nothing was wrong with him, he would call for Dr. Behar, an allergist from Argentina who understood him better than anyone else.

"What's wrong, Flavio?" Behar would ask.

"My feet," Flavio would answer.

Behar would inspect his feet, saying each time, "They are fine, Flavio, just fine."

"*Gracias, gracias,*" Flavio would answer with a grin. And the doctor would pat his shoulder and leave, knowing that very soon he might be called again.

For Flavio the following days were to be trying ones, filled as they were with blood tests, sweat tests, tuberculin and pulmonary function studies, tests to rule out syphilis, ova and parasite tests, and X-ray studies of his chest and bone structure. To best cope with the multiple nature of his problems, each doctor on Dr. Falliers's team studied Flavio from the vantage point of his own specialty. They would then combine their findings and analyze them as a whole to determine the best way to treat him. Their preliminary analyses found Flavio allergic to wool, pyrethrum, birch tree, Western wheat, and a number of other things.

To Flavio the frequent tests were painful, and because of his innate modesty, offensive. After one extremely difficult series José Gallo found him weeping disconsolately at a hospital window as he watched the rain pour down, as it often did in the favela. "Cheer up, Flavio. You must think about the future. All of this is to make you a well boy," José had advised him. Flavio remained quiet for several moments; then, wiping at his tears, he smiled and said, "You know what? I'd like to drive a big airplane and fly like a bird someday." Such were the new dreams of a child who up to now had reason to dream only of death.

Flavio's psychological and intelligence tests presented another kind of problem since they had been standardized on American school children. Despite the language barrier and his lack of schooling, he was able to grasp the pantomime directions given him and to do what the examiner asked. He reacted to mechanical things far better than he did to verbal things, and his facial expressions indicated that he knew when he succeeded or failed. When given the Rorschach test, in which he was shown ten inkblot designs to find out what image or emotion each design evoked, Flavio's responses were bland; he perceived vague forms and colors like those of blood or clouds.

Many of his errors were what psychologists call "good errors." Arithmetic was difficult but he learned to manipulate numbers rather well. These tests revealed that he had a surprisingly large fund of general knowledge, but the most positive thing they found out about him was his ability to stick with a problem, no matter how difficult it was. It was finally determined that he could function at the level of a nine-year-old American child. Considering his favela background, this wasn't bad.

These results, however, were but a minimal sample of his behavior. He was found to be alert, interested in his surroundings, capable of absorbing his new environment, learning adequate English, and adjusting to school. So that his transitional period would be easy as possible, a local Portuguese family was located in Denver for Flavio to converse with. Jose Gonçalves, his wife Kathy, and their two older sons, ten-year-old Rick and Mark, eight, all spoke English and Portuguese. After Kathy Gonçalves came to see Flavio several times while he was in the hospital, it was arranged for him to spend weekends and holidays with her family.

No one on the staff expected any more than a willingness from Flavio and nothing less than a supreme effort from themselves. Everyone from the janitor to the director wanted to make his sojourn a happy one. Jimmy Gaddy, a easy going lanky boy of fourteen and Flavio's first friend, bought a Portuguese phrase book in hopes of getting closer to Flavio. Tommy Ebbe, who was only seven, walked over to him on the third day, and unable to break the language barrier, pleaded, "Will you be my friend, Flavio? Say yes." And though the words meant nothing to him, Flavio understood Tommy's hand on his shoulder. It was Jimmy and Tommy who took him by the hand that first week and led him to the playground, the cafeteria, and the dormitories where he met other boys and girls. And although Flavio was tense and suspicous he accepted their help. They taught him a few basic words such as "hello," "friend," "baseball," and "television." One day, perhaps to show his appreciation, Flavio got permission to cook black beans and rice for Tommy, Jimmy, and a few other boys. The beans took a long time to come to a boil because of the high altitude and caused Flavio some slight embarrassment. "These beans are taking too long to cook," he complained to José. This treat went over so big with Jimmy and Tommy they asked that he be allowed to cook every week.

On the eighth day, after it was determined that he was not tubercular, Flavio was moved out of the hospital to Boy's Cottage, a dormitory for boys of his age. But soon enough it became clear that he wouldn't get along there. The boys at the cottage were more mature, larger, and rougher. They innocently teased Flavio because he couldn't speak English and because he was so small for his age. The boys meant no harm, but Flavio misunderstood, and by the third day he had been in two fights in which he used a favela technique of jabbing for the eyes with his fingers to defend himself. Each day after, he became more sullen, angry, and unmanageable. He resisted going to the hospital for his tests and became hostile and disobedient to the staff. Though everyone tried, no one, including José Gallo and Dr. Behar, could get through to him. Suddenly, Flavio began wheezing and coughing again, and finding it harder to breathe. Before long he was back in the hospital.

At the end of the first two weeks it was time for José Gallo to return to Brazil. And though he realized things would be immeasurably better for Flavio, he secretly feared that the problems facing both Flavio and those who would save him were insuperable. He was hopeful but skeptical; the predictions of the Brazilian doctor who had examined Flavio still gnawed at him. José, probably more than anyone, knew the great difference that lay between Flavio's new home and the one he had left. He couldn't help but wonder if everyone who would be directly involved with him understood just how badly the favela had ravaged his mind and body. So José's last days were spent bolstering Flavio's spirit and preparing him for the difficult months ahead, stressing the importance of his learning to appreciate what others were trying to do for him, and not least to remember that Brazil was his real home. "You are Brazilian and we expect good things from you; so you must not disappoint us. Understand?"

"Yes," Flavio answered with a nod of his head. He had become extremely apprehensive about José's leaving. "No one around here will understand what I say," he complained. "It is terrible sometimes with those awful needles and nasty medicine they give me. I don't want to cry like a baby but it sure does hurt."

"But they are doing all this to make you well. You must remember that and be brave. The Gonçalves family will be here to explain things for you. There is also Dr. Behar who will be with you."

But Flavio now claimed that neither he nor Dr. Behar understood one another. "That doctor speaks very bad Portuguese," he said. Actually the good doctor spoke Spanish.

On the morning José left, Flavio sent with him some of the gifts he had received to his brothers and sisters. "Tell my family that I love them and miss them, and that I will come home well," he said after his spirits had lifted somewhat. But by nightfall he felt desperately alone, and he cried a good part of the night and suffered a mild attack the following morning. After a few days, he was on the mend again, and he was sent back to Boy's Cottage. But when his troubles started all over again, Dr. Falliers decided to move him to the Willens building, a dormitory where younger boys lived.

Flavio's tantrums peaked on the Friday afternoon he was to move, and he chased a couple of girls with his knife. Dr. Behar was called. He thought for a moment, and seeing that Flavio had reinforced his arsenal with a broomstick, he hastily telephoned for Kathy Gonçalves. "It's urgent," he said to her. "Get over here right away."

By the time Kathy Gonçalves arrived Flavio had become

hysterical and, backed against a wall, he was standing everyone off with the knife and broomstick. After about ten minutes of coaxing she got the knife away from him, put him in her car and drove him to her home. When they arrived he was so angry he picked up a toy gun and slammed it against the door. Kathy slapped him. "If you want to live by the rules of the favela they will send you back there, Flavio da Silva!" she warned him. Flavio quieted down then. The favela was the last place he wanted to return to.

By now Flavio had been at the Institute for nearly a month. But despite the general goodwill that had been directed toward him, Dick and Gwen Rackett, house parents in the Willens building, were concerned when they heard that he would be moving in with them. They felt he had received too much attention in the press, and might have become spoiled by the gifts and letters showered upon him from the outside. They were also worried about how the other boys at Willens would accept him. Just before he was permanently assigned to them, they had overheard a conversation between Mitsu, a Japanese boy, and his friend Ronny. Said Mitsu the Buddhist, "That's what I hate about church. It says we have to love everybody, and I sure don't love Flavio."

"Well, my family is poor too," said Ronny, "and nobody puts my picture in *Life* magazine and sends me toys and lots of crappy letters."

"He's a spoiled brat," Mitsu further complained. "You'd think he was a God or something the way everybody goes on over him."

Flavio moved in one Monday morning. And in his first week at Willens he seemed to live up to Mitsu's billing. He unabashedly walked into Mitsu's cubicle one day and took his pencil sharpener. Six of Ronny's prized pencils accompanied the sharpener. His raids on the personal property of others in the building were made with a calm that astounded the Racketts. Since Flavio couldn't speak English, they became more and more frustrated in their attempts to reprimand him.

"Flav, stealing isn't part of our culture," Gwen would find herself saying, only to realize that Flavio hadn't understood a word she had spoken. Even more puzzling to her was his look of wonderment and his engaging smile. It was strange, she thought, that he never tried to conceal his contraband. He always kept it in open display on the table next to his bed. Strange too, she thought, was his giving some of his gifts to others who hadn't asked for them. Some of his transgressions were amusing. When the boys at Willens were encouraged to build a coin collection, his was the largest and was put together the quickest. Then it was discovered that he had filled the slots in his cardboard coin containers by taking the other boys' coins from their bureaus, banks, and jeans.

Dick and Gwen Rackett were in their early thirties, blond and good looking. They were also warm individuals who wanted to help the children at the Institute. Like all the other house parents hired there, they had some previous experience in child care, but were not required to have a college education or any psychological training; a warm and caring attitude was the main prerequisite. All the house parents had separate residential quarters in the same dormitories in which the children lived. They were trained to watch out for infections, blisters, sore throats, and any signs of possible asthmatic attacks. If, in the middle of the night, an attack did occur, they took the child to the hospital. Twenty-six children lived in the building in individual cubicles separated by partitions and equipped with beds, desks, clothes closets, and chests of drawers. The dormitory had a large central recreational room furnished with sofas, lounge chairs, tables of reading materials, a radio, and a television set. The hardwood floors were kept scrupulously clean and free of all carpeting to avoid any dust which might set off an attack.

The children were grouped together in dormitories according to their age. Flavio was the exception. At twelve, he was three years older than any other boy at Willens. Only a third of the population at the Institute consisted of girls. Girls, it seems, accepted home treatment more easily than boys, who generally resented giving up rigorous sports like basketball, track, or football. In an attempt to keep things normal, Dick Rackett planned regular athletic activities for the boys. Only a medical directive could prevent their participation. For some, Willens was like home. For Flavio it was, without doubt, better than home.

After a week there, Flavio had mastered a few English sentences, most of them slang and of a nature Gwen Rackett couldn't bring herself to repeat. But she noticed that he was taking less from the other boys. She felt encouraged by this until Guy, a little black boy, complained that his radio was missing. After a quick search Gwen found the radio in plain sight on Flavio's desk, and this confirmed her suspicion that Flavio didn't realize that he had done something wrong. Gwen didn't mention the radio's disappearance, nor did she accuse Flavio of stealing it when he brought it to her, saying that it had been given to him. When he asked her to put his name on it she unhesitatingly wrote his name on a piece of tape and stuck it on the radio. Then she watched him for a couple of days.

Finally Guy asked that something be done immediately. He was now in the hospital with a seizure, and wanted his radio for company. Gwen, without pressing the point, tried with some difficulty to make Flavio understand that the radio belonged to Guy. She left him feeling that she hadn't gotten through. Several hours later she walked past Guy's cubicle and looked in. There was the radio. Flavio had removed the tape and replaced the radio on Guy's desk.

Gwen reveled at that act. She hoped that she was finally

beginning to better understand him. But there were still so many things to set right with Flavio. She found his table manners abominable, and she was distressed by the other boys' teasing him about his eating habits. No matter that his shack in the favela didn't have a table or silverware to put on it. He must learn now, she insisted, to use a knife and fork, to stir tea with a spoon instead of a pocket knife. He would have to stop picking up meat with his fingers and gobbling it down before cutting it. She would have to break his habit of going to bed so late and stalling in bed the next morning when everyone else was up. Meanwhile she was beginning to wonder why Flavio was closing himself off more and more from the others.

One could assume that since he had never been loved, he didn't know how to accept love. But there was more to it than that. Walled off behind the language barrier, he must have felt himself to be in enemy territory, mistaking a friendly smile for mockery and a pat on the back for a hostile act. During periods of depression he would go off and stand alone with the blade of his pocket knife open. He often became morose and uncommunicative. To Gwen it was like trying to open a door that didn't exist. Despite her growing affection for him, the truth turned up in her diary: "Flavio da Silva remains, after the first two weeks, belligerent, resistant to discipline, and uncontrollable."

During those two weeks he had gone to the infirmary four times, twice for vomiting and twice for severe asthmatic attacks. The asthma responded promptly to treatment, and Dr. Falliers felt confident that they had his medical problems in hand. But Flavio's psychological problems were still out of control, and he seemed to be showing very little improvement. His moods, shifting from one course to another, remained a baffling complex of hostility, joy, despair, and loneliness.

Eight

Flavio was to enter school for the first time in his life in September of 1961. Being twelve, he had a lot of catching up to do. So, with his health stabilized, steps were taken to prepare him for the first grade. Virginia Hansen, the motherly, energetic principal of Cheltenham, the school he would attend, occasionally came to the Institute to help him with English. To enlarge his vocabulary she would show him objects he was familiar with, like onions, pencils, baseballs, apples, books, or perhaps a water glass. After identifying these objects aloud she would have Flavio repeat their names in English. Miss Hansen was astounded at the speed with which he caught on and enjoyed working with him, but as a school principal, her time was limited. Since there was so little time left before school began, there was urgent need for a full-time instructor to take over. Kathy Gonçalves was the likely choice, since she liked Flavio

and Flavio liked her; so *Life* magazine immediately hired her
to start teaching him English.

It was mid-July. Less than two months remained before
school would begin, but Kathy, a dynamic young woman, was
determined to have Flavio ready for enrollment by September.
Each day, starting about ten in the morning, she spent an hour
at the Institute with Flavio, using flash cards, newspaper head-
lines, magazine captions, and English and Portuguese comic
books to drill the meaning of words and sentences into him; she
used a tape measure to help him recognize and evaluate the
difference between numbers. These lessons were all impro-
vised and continued into the weekends when she took him
home. Kathy hoped that living with her own family might help
Flavio to better understand the communal nature of dormitory
living. She also wanted to create meaningful experiences for
him, then give him a vocabulary to describe those experiences
in English and in Portuguese.

Flavio's Portuguese was a kind of gutter argot—broken and
full of favela slang that was almost incomprehensible to a
middle-class Brazilian. Knowing that he would return to Brazil
eventually, Kathy decided on her own to teach him Portuguese
as well. If Flavio was to have a better life when he went home,
Kathy felt his Portuguese would have to be drastically improved, and with furious zeal she set out to help him catch up
with everything that had been denied him.

Besides tutoring him in languages, Kathy coached Flavio in
arithmetic and good manners. She also tried to give him the
values that most children acquire as a birthright and to imbue
him with long-term ambitions and goals. It was second nature
for a middle-class boy like one of her own sons to invest effort
in something that would pay off in ten years, but a boy like
Flavio was used to thinking only in terms of immediate rewards. He lacked motivation and didn't yet understand the importance of education. But Kathy was encouraged by his native

intelligence and his ability to learn so rapidly. "He's like dry soil soaking up everything around him," she told her husband after one weekend session with Flavio. And she was seized with a blazing fervor to prepare him, not just for the first grade, but for life itself.

José Gonçalves taught languages at the University of Denver, and he knew how difficult it was to grasp a foreign language under emotional strain. At ten, without knowing a word of English, he had been sent from his home in Portugal to a boarding school in South Africa. Secure, well adjusted, and fresh from the heart of an upper middle-class family, he nevertheless found the language barrier distressing. Now he could sympathize with Flavio and his problems which were, by far, greater than his had been.

José and Kathy, a Denver girl, first met at a picnic in the summer of 1948 while they were both students, he at the University of Denver and she at the University of Missouri. The tall, blondish Kathy was immediately smitten with José's charm and swarthy good looks. They both spoke Spanish fluently, and shortly after their courtship blossomed, José taught her Portuguese. They were married in 1950 and moved into a six-room clapboard bungalow located on the west side of Denver. It was a comfortable home, simply furnished, and located in the middle of a tree-lined block. It was to this same home, about ten miles from the Institute, that Kathy took Flavio each weekend. Neil, the youngest son, and Flavio shared a bedroom lined with bookshelves, and with a long table holding a handsome display of miniature airplane, automobile, and boat models. Flavio was happy there, and before long he took on the kind of responsibilities that he had assumed in his shack in the favela. He looked after the three-year-old Neil, picked up after himself, helped wash dishes, and did part of the housework. José became as devoted to his welfare as he was to that of his own sons, and Kathy cared for him like a mother, while Mark, Rick, and Neil thought of him as their own brother. The weekends he spent with them were good ones.

This made it all the more baffling when, after the third week of his association with the Gonçalves family, Flavio suddenly lapsed into another series of misdemeanors at the Institute. He refused to talk, eat, or go to bed at the right hour. The nurses couldn't get a thermometer into his mouth for temperature readings, and he threw everything—bread crusts, orange peelings, apple cores, nut shells—on the floor.

Within a few days Gwen Rackett's patience with Flavio gave out. In desperation she cornered the doctors during their daily visits to the Willens building, describing her confrontations with Flavio, his feuding with the other children, his roaming the dormitory after bedtime, his rejection of house rules, and his offensive behavior in the cafeteria. "He has become a real demon again," she complained to Dr. Falliers.

Doctors Bukantz, Falliers, Behar, and the staff psychiatrists met to try to get to the bottom of the trouble. A thorough investigation left everyone perplexed. There was no evidence of any medical or social imbalance to justify Flavio's sudden relapse. Flavio, without his knowing it, was put under closer observation, and he was brought back to the hospital to sleep each night. There he became even more sullen and uncommunicative and started wheezing and coughing again.

On one Friday afternoon, moments before Kathy Gonçalves was to pick him up for the weekend, Flavio, provoked by teasing, grabbed a pole used for raising windows and chased Mitsu and another boy into the Racketts' living quarters. Kathy arrived just in time to quell his anger. Leading him to her car she heard Gwen shout, "I'm glad you're taking him! That boy is becoming a terrible nuisance to all of us! I'm really sorry sometimes that they brought him here!"

Kathy was incensed at this outburst but she ignored it; during the ride home she lectured Flavio sternly, telling him that he was surely going to end up back at the favela. On Sunday afternoon the family took him on a motor trip to the Colorado foothills. Maybe the mountain air cooled him off, or perhaps he took Kathy's warning seriously; no one really knew. In any event, Flavio's behavior as well as his wheezing and coughing took a turn for the better the following week and no one welcomed the change more than Gwen and Dick Rackett.

In September Flavio was enrolled at Cheltenham, a Denver public elementary school. Cheltenham was a huge, ancient, two-storied redbrick building located four blocks from the Institute. It was a good school and within easy walking distance of the Willens building. Flavio's first morning there was unnerving. Having misunderstood his directions, he wandered about, jostled by swarms of jabbering strangers, with a paper on which the correct room number was written clutched in his hand. Then suddenly a shrill bell sounded, and in the next few seconds the cavernous hallway was empty. He was alone and lost. A janitor found him roaming about and took him into Eleanor Massey's first-grade classroom ten minutes after class had begun. Eleanor welcomed him and introduced him to his classmates and showed him to his desk. Ignoring everyone around him, Flavio took a pencil and started drawing unrecognizable figures on a pad. Eleanor Massey watched him for a moment, considered stopping him, thought better of it, and went on teaching.

It was a big room with a twenty-foot-high ceiling. Vertical oak paneling covered the lower walls beneath the blackboards and north windows down to the polished hardwood floors. Thirty-one wooden desks with sunken inkwells accommodated the students who made up the class. In the back of the room as well as in the outer corridors, long lines of ornate brass hooks were screwed into the walls, and on these the students hung their wraps. "I like that place. I like it but it's crazy," Flavio confided to Gwen Rackett when he returned to the Institute for lunch.

"What do you like about it?" Gwen had asked.

"Oh, I don't know. It's just crazy-like."

"Is it the other children, or the teacher?"

"The teacher is okay. She's good. But those kids are too little. Why do I have to be around kids so little?"

Gwen knew the answer but she didn't give it to him. Although he was not much bigger in size than the six-year-olds who were his classmates, he obviously felt he had little in common with them. By the end of the first week the sudden shift of authority, plus the formality of the classroom, was beginning to frustrate him, and within a fortnight Flavio had totally withdrawn from his classmates. He wouldn't speak or play with them and stayed by himself making drawings. His pencils, crayons, and paper became his treasures. He often refused to leave his desk at lunch time. During recess he would cram the pencils and crayons into his pockets and stuff the tablet in his shirt. Off alone in one corner of the playground, he watched his classmates at play and met all their overtures toward friendship with silence. Nevertheless, the children persisted—Flavio was something of a novelty to them; they were fascinated with his drawings because his people always resembled animals. He seemed afraid to use more than one color at a time. He became increasingly compulsive and hated being interrupted, even by Eleanor Massey. If she was reading to the class and the bell rang, he would insist upon her finishing. If he had been drawing, he would become upset if he couldn't finish before going on to the next class. And Flavio took extreme pride in his work; patiently, Eleanor used this pride to combat his loneliness and inner tensions. She encouraged and praised his efforts, pushing, coaxing, and guiding him over the rough spots. In less than two months, he had mastered the letters of the vocabulary and could read and understand an astounding number of sentences.

But Flavio's rebuffs eventually had an effect on the other children, and they stopped trying to talk with him or inviting him to participate in their play. Eleanor Massey sensed his loneliness but felt helpless to do anything about it. Experience told her that when Flavio tired of being a loner, it would be up to him to do something about it, and there were signs that he was tiring. One day as sides were being chosen for a ballgame he stepped up and demanded to play. It wasn't a very gracious way to ask for acceptance, but he was allowed to play and partially redeemed himself by hitting two home runs. He further improved his status one day by picking up an injured child and carrying him to the main office for treatment.

A little girl named Sonia, newly arrived from Brazil, turned out to be the agent of his major breakthrough. She had been in the classroom for just a few minutes when Flavio realized she couldn't speak English. Jumping up he rushed over to Sonia to translate and explain Eleanor Massey's instructions. From then on he helped in many ways, explaining to Sonia what the next day's lesson would be, and acting as a general interpreter for her and Eleanor Massey. Almost immediately he became more popular and better liked by the other children. He then began sharing his pencils, crayons, and ideas about his drawings.

"Why does that boy you're drawing have a tail like a monkey?" a kid named Mickey Conway asked him.

"Why? Because all you boys got tails just like monkeys," Flavio answered, much to the amusement of the class.

Emerging now from his shell, Flavio was revealing another talent. He was a comic, an outright ham. He got to the point where he could imitate almost anything or anybody in the class. "Look!" he would say, scratching his behind, "this is Jimmy Mason with fleas in his pocket!" He could keep the class in stitches for ten or fifteen minutes at a time. It became a game with the children to figure out who could get him to tell the funniest story. The class favorite was a story he made up about a black elephant who died and went to heaven but got kicked out because he wouldn't wear white wings.

Flavio's academic work improved along with his attitudes. He wanted his writing to be perfect, and he hated making errors; they made him unhappy and he would bang his fist on the desk as soon as he spotted one. He also loved to tease. One day he was pounding his paper with the point of his crayon, trying to make rain. Eleanor put her finger to her mouth. "Shush," she said. A short time later she was drawing a chart with a squeaky felt pen. And Flavio, with a big grin on his face, put his finger to his mouth. "Shush," he repeated to Eleanor. His humor was his saving grace, and it helped his classmates to eventually accept him and love him. Now when he did something wrong or something he felt was stupid, he would laugh outloud at himself. And whereas he used to hate criticism in the beginning, he now accepted it remarkably well. Flavio was growing more handsome by the day, and all the little girls in the rhythm class liked to dance with him. He gave the class its biggest treat one afternoon by dancing the samba the way they danced it in the favela.

From his very first day in class, Eleanor Massey felt that Flavio had average intelligence, but this was only a guess. He was so intellectually deprived when he arrived it was difficult for her to determine. But now he had done better than she had dared to hope. At the first quarter's end she graded his art, considerably improved, and his other nine subjects, ranging from arithmetic to science, satisfactory. At the bottom of the report she commented, "Flavio is a gem."

Flavio's five-month medical report was also encouraging. He had gained five pounds and grown three-fourths of an inch, the asthma attacks had all but stopped, and by mid-

December he had been taken off all medication. His behavior at the Willens building had also improved, his temper tantrums came less frequently now, and he was getting along much better with the Racketts and his dormitory mates, although he still shied away from close relationships with them.

Gradually the protectiveness Flavio had shown for his family developed in his attitudes toward the children at Willens. At nearly thirteen he was by far the oldest child in the dormitory; the others were between seven and ten. One night when everyone was asleep, Mitsu, the Japanese boy who had mentioned his dislike for Flavio, and whom Flavio had chased with the window stick, began wheezing loudly. When he grew steadily worse Flavio got up, dressed Mitsu, and carried him to the hospital. Then one day he walked up to Gwen and volunteered to be a waiter in the dining room. Suddenly it seemed that he was again carrying out a need to do things for other people. Gradually, the Racketts discerned an improvement in his English. "I think he understands much more than we imagined," she told Dr. Falliers. "It's amazing. He is suddenly showing a wonderful sense of humor, mimicking and using American slang like the other boys."

The Racketts had an aquarium with some rather expensive fish in it. Flavio liked the forty-cent catfish best because they were more active. One night he went to their quarters with some sort of loudspeaker arrangement and began counting the fish.

"You're frightening them, Flavio," Gwen said. He looked up and smiled, then began whispering, "One, two, three," and so on until he had accounted for every fish. The Racketts then realized he was showing them how well he could count in English. Gwen was beginning to like him more each day. She noticed that he was looking much healthier, that his color was good, and that he was gaining weight; she was happy that at last she was getting through to him. "We'll soon have a number one American boy at Willens," she told Dick later that night.

Flavio was never too enthusiastic about homework. He seemed to enjoy better going off for his English and Portuguese lessons with Kathy and visiting her three sons. He had his first real Christmas with them, happily absorbed in all the legendary fantasies of the holiday he had never enjoyed before. He slept restlessly on Christmas Eve, hoping to hear reindeer hooves on the roof, tinkling bells outside his window, and *Papai Noel* squeezing himself down the chimney in his bright red suit. After he had at last fallen asleep Kathy and José Gonçalves slipped quietly into the living room and filled his stockings with candy and nuts; they spread his presents under the big tree the boys and Flavio had decorated a week before. When early the next morning he was awakened and led into the magical room, he was wonder-struck.

Flavio received gifts not only from the Gonçalves family but also from many *Life* readers who had not forgotten him on this day: two transistor radios, water colors, blue jeans, a set of matched marbles, new shoes, three ties, a water pistol, a billfold, fountain pen, socks, a hat, a baseball and glove, and money. Grinning broadly, he sat on the floor in his pajamas amid the presents and wrappings, perhaps convinced at last that there was indeed a *Papai Noel*. He had put on one shoe, his new hat, and the baseball glove when suddenly he remembered something. Jumping up he hobbled into his bedroom and returned with a beautifully wrapped package which he handed to Kathy Gonçalves. She opened it, looked, then grabbed Flavio and hugged him. "Just what we need for breakfast!" she exclaimed, holding up a package of sweet rolls.

At noon Kathy's parents arrived with more gifts, and Flavio shared a surprise with Rick, Mark, and Neil. Their grandfather had brought them a large plastic boat. Afterward, leaves were added to the dining room table and everyone sat down to dinner. There was a big roast turkey with stuffing, cranberry sauce, candied sweet potatoes, spinach, apple pie and ice cream. Later they went sledding, and finally everyone piled into cars for a trip to one of Colorado's spectacular canyons. It was Flavio da Silva's first real Christmas and it was glorious, one that he would long remember.

Flavio was adjusting well to his new environment, but he missed his brothers and sisters and often felt his separation from them keenly. In the early part of the new year he wrapped some of his gifts to send to them—one of the transistor radios, water colors, marbles, and the water pistol. The deepest gloom settled over him when he sat alone watching the other children enjoy weekly letters from their families. He wondered about those whom he loved and had left behind. Who minded Zacarias now that he wasn't there? Did Maria do the cooking? Were she and Mario still kicking each other's shins and knocking the other kids around? Had there been anything to his father's suspicions that all of them might get kicked out of the new house after he was taken to America? Those magical hours in the new house had been too fleeting, too overwhelming for him to fix in his mind—sometimes he still thought of his family as living in the favela. And why didn't he get letters from home like the others? Flavio certainly knew why, but it was hard for him to accept the truth.

Kathy Gonçalves wrote Ruth Fowler at *Life* magazine in New York saying that he was lonely, that he was becoming upset because he had not heard from his family since he had left Brazil, and that he was getting a lot of attention and affection, but not enough to replace the love of his family.

Ruth Fowler wrote back:

One of the difficulties of keeping Flavio supplied with information about his family is their unresponsiveness because of the load they carry in relation to all of the other children. Neither the mother nor the father read or write, and I am afraid the father is primarily interested in Flavio's good "fortune." It therefore makes it doubly difficult to gather information about the individual brothers and sisters, unless José Gallo can take some of his already limited time to do so. I am confident he will keep in touch with Flavio as much as he can for he really loves this small Brazilian boy.

Shortly after, word from the family came via cable through José Gallo for Flavio. It read:

WE MISS YOU AND WE HOPE YOU ARE GETTING WELL AND WE LOVE YOU. YOU HAVE A NEW BABY SISTER. HER NAME IS CELIA.

Nair had named her ninth child for José Gallo's wife. It had been born in July. By now it was over five months old.

Nine

Back in Rio, the Da Silva family had begun to settle into their new life, and things were better than they had ever been for Nair da Silva. With more rest than she had enjoyed in her adult life, her cheeks began to fill out and she smiled now and then. The children seemed happy in their new surroundings, and they were healthy. They played in their paved back yard with the toys they had been given on their visit to Sears Roebuck. Maria, Mario, and Luzia, the three oldest, had been enrolled in the first grade at the Lia Braga Farias Primary School, which was only a hundred yards from their home. But they would have to enter the following semester because there were no vacancies. They could have gone to a school a mile away but José da Silva did not want them to cross the highway that lay between the house and the school.

"We want our children to go to school," José said, "but it's best for them to wait a little instead of getting killed on that speedway. All of them will go to school as soon as they're big enough."

Removed from the oppressive favela atmosphere, the children were more gentle with one another. They still fought, but less often, and they no longer needed to grab hungrily at one another's food. Still it was clear that the adjustment to a new way of life after the favela's squalid shack existence was going to take time. Isabel fell in love with the bidet and was constantly trying to bathe in it. One morning, much to their mother's dismay, Maria and Batista ran streamers of toilet paper from the bathroom to all parts of the house and onto the porch. The children still threw their clothes into piles instead of hanging them up in the wardrobe closets. By the fifth day the toilet had been hopelessly clogged with things that should have gone into the garbage bin. But as Nair learned the ropes, so did her children, and before long even the toothbrushes were being used because the children enjoyed watching the water flow out of the tap. However, three-year-old Albia became mysteriously ill because the toothpaste was so palatable that she was swallowing it in chunks. Now Nair had them in the pajamas for bed each night and she made each child take a shower once a day. She washed their clothes daily and pressed them with her new iron. She loved that iron; it was the first she had owned in her life. She used it religiously.

Nair was now relieved of Flavio's tortured nights of wheezing and coughing, of her fear of the death that she always felt creeping up on him. She rejoiced in the fact that, unlike herself, her children would one day be able to read and write. During that July, after an easy labor, she had given birth to Celia Nair. That birth, unlike the others, was a pleasure to her. For the first time she had been given prenatal care and had taken calcium tablets and other diet supplements. And for the first time she had been relaxed when her labor began; afterward she had been able to recuperate at the hospital for several days—a new experience indeed for her.

Nair had first moved into the favela with her family when she was only ten years old. She had worked as a scullery girl in wealthy Copacabana homes until she was twenty-eight. At that age she had borne Flavio, and a couple of years later, Maria. Now, at forty, she was at last making a real home for her children.

"This is what I have always wanted," she confided to José Gallo. "It's easy compared to the favela, even with Flavio gone. I don't have to carry water up that awful hill anymore and scrounge around for wood to make cooking fires. I'm only washing for my own now. I'm lucky; I want my children to benefit. The main thing we miss now is Flavio. But if he is in good hands he will come back to us well. I pray each day that he will."

José da Silva, convinced at last that this property was truly his, settled easily into the pleasure it offered. At times he would walk to the end of his block, turn about; then, with unpracticed casualness, walk back toward it admiring its beauty and the fact that it belonged to him. His reluctance to express himself was all but gone; he was suddenly as voluble as a parrot, and his moods were no longer so morose. José could even have been accused of being cheerful at times. There was less thumping on the children's heads, and he now occasionally told them jokes or tales he remembered from his childhood in northeast Brazil. The children particularly liked one grisly story about the giant-sized, greasy-purple women who come up from the ocean depths at night to hunt down bad children, whom they ate for supper. Bustling with new energy and hope, Da Silva moved his brother Julio and his wife into the back cottage. Working evenings and weekends, he helped Julio replace all the cracked tiles and rotted roof timbers on the cottage. Within a week it was dry and habitable. José and Julio then sold their favela shacks for 30,000 cruzeiros ($120 each), payable in ten monthly installments of 3,000 cruzeiros each. They repainted José's favela kerosene stall with leftover paint from the house and put it up for sale at 90,000 cruzeiros ($300). But after waiting for two months they were offered only half that much. Consequently, José restocked it and decided to keep it until he got a better offer. Sometimes the two brothers would sit on the counter of the stall shaking their heads in wonderment at José's turn of luck.

With everything else going so well, José was still concerned about his three oldest children starting in the first grade at such advanced ages. He feared the other children would make fun of them. But when he enrolled them the schoolmistress told him that he shouldn't worry, showing him other children of the same age or even older who were also just starting school. "They will learn fast and get ahead here. There will be many nice friends for them," she assured José. And José had felt reassured, for this place was, in comparison to the favela, an oasis of peace and friendliness. It was no longer a cutthroat struggle just to survive.

José easily persuaded *Life* to help him purchase a 1946 Chevrolet truck. *Life* was to pay half the purchase price; José was to pay the other half out of his earnings. The remainder of the fund set up for the family, which by now was about $4,000, was to be held in reserve for repairs, José's failure to make monthly payments, or any other contingencies. Trucking, he had explained, was the one thing he wanted to do most. And he had it all figured out. By making pickups and deliveries for nearby stores and small plants, he and Julio could clear 45,000 cruzeiros ($150) monthly net profit. With the truck they could pay for light and gas and still make a decent living. The truck had arrived on one Friday afternoon, completely overhauled and repainted blue with all parts in fine working order. It had cost 220,000 cruzeiros (about $750). José spent a good part of

that weekend admiring his new acquisition and pointing out its
features to his neighbors. "Look at her, five tons, six cylinders
and a motor with the power of eighty-five horses."

Quipped one neighbor, "Someday you'll be running a fleet
of them between Rio and the backlands, José." The man had
spoken in jest, but José, filled now with optimism and the reality of his current good fortune, gave serious thought to the
man's words. "Perhaps, perhaps. It is possible," he answered.
But for the present, first things had to come first. He had to get
some jobs and make some money for those monthly payments.
On Sunday afternoon he piled the entire family into the truck
for a joy ride. They headed first for the favela of Catacumba. It
was natural that a drive past that place would provide him with
his proudest moment.

The following week José began lining up hauling contracts
with the local shops and factories. A neighboring trucker, with
a smaller and older truck, was netting some 40,000 cruzeiros a
month. José, it seemed, should do even better. However, one
serious problem remained—José's chronic lethargy. It was no
secret that he preferred to let Julio do the hauling while he, the
owner, sat still and split the proceeds. In any event, José Manuel da Silva was now a trucker and, as he so proudly put it, "the
president of his firm."

A third of the money which was sent in by *Life's* readers had
been set aside for the favela. That fund would come to about
$10,000. This looked pitiful in the face of the enormous backlog
of needs that had to be met there. Catacumba needed the most
basic kinds of services. The muddy paths had to be paved; the
open sewers covered over and the whole network expanded;
electricity and water had to be brought in. In addition, the
favelados wanted a police station to help control the dope ped-
dlers and criminals who terrorized Catacumba. They also
needed a community building which could house a child care

center, medical and maternity clinics, and provide a place where literacy classes and civic meetings could be held.

Divided among the population of the favela, the funds amounted to approximately fifty cents per person. Accomplishing any real improvement with this tiny sum seemed hopeless. But the *Life* stories had had an effect. Businessmen throughout the area offered supplies at cost, and clubs and civic groups offered financial support and man-hours of work. individual doctors and social workers volunteered their services. The people of Rio were at last responding to Catacumba's needs.

But the favelados, with the help and encouragement of José Gallo, turned out to be the crucial factor. They formed an association, elected officers, appointed committees and a straw boss. They drew up estimates for cement, gravel, sand, bricks, and for electricity to permit night work. Alleys and pathways would be paved by crews who lived adjacent to them, in hopes that this would stimulate competition through pride and achievement and speed the work along.

Further plans called for pumps to hoist water thousands of feet to new reservoirs at the top of Catacumba, a brick, constantly-burning incinerator to eliminate tons of favela garbage that the city of Rio refused to collect, and finally a community center through which to register all favela families, distribute surplus food, initiate clean-up, health, and educational campaigns. The plans were many and grand.

One bright Saturday morning two trucks screeched to a halt at the entrance to the favela and dumped the first loads of building materials. The eager favelados gathered around and watched. At their feet were enough supplies for eight days of work. Shortly after, Carlos Lacerda, the new Governor of Guanabara State, wrote to tell Ruth Fowler that what was happening there was a good thing. "It is impossible," he said, "to move out all the favela dwellers, even if they have enough down-payment money for another home. There is not enough low-cost housing to move them into." Lacerda was right. In Rio alone there were close to 700,000 favelados in its 205 favelas, with fewer than 7,000 low-cost homes available or planned.

The work moved on. By October the favela project was in high gear. The Society of Catacumba Dwellers, complete with a women's auxiliary, was named and legally registered. With a burst of energy, in a single weekend, it built a community center with an extra storehouse for tools and building materials. Cimento Maua, a cement company, delivered 1,100 sacks of cement at a 33% discount to pave the four main alleys. The paving began the next weekend with four crews joyously racing each other to the hilltop. For the first time in Catacumba, a public telephone and power line were installed at the bottom of the hill, and the power was run up the hill for night work in the alleys.

With so much energy already in motion the favelados were cheered on by the promise of further outside help. Armo Steel offered substantial discounts on culverts for sewers to be installed along side the alleys. The water department offered to draw up engineering plans and blue prints for a water supply system. All this would coincide with the plans to install garbage collection centers and incinerators for garbage disposal. The *Pioneiras Sociais,* a voluntary health organization headed by the Governor's wife, promised medical crews for an all-out campaign to wipe out endemic diseases once the basic sanitary facilities were completed. Then one morning José Gallo got a call from an official of the American Society, a group made up of American families living in Rio. They were eager, she said, to donate clothing and other services that might be needed. *Life's* Rio Bureau was certain that U.S. surplus foods and dried milk could be obtained for distribution through the newly erected community center.

Flavio's favela, financed by people-to-people contributions, had miraculously turned into a self-help project. The idea that a community should be involved in its own development was so simple as to be revolutionary. Apparently no one concerned with the problems of the favelas had ever thought of using it before.

If the project had an individual father it was José Gallo. The Society of Catacumba Dwellers met every Tuesday and Thursday. José was at every meeting, doing everything from planning to settling fist fights. He was the main link of communication between Ruth Fowler, who controlled the funds, and the operation in Rio. To make sound judgments from such a great distance, Ruth needed sound guidance. It was José, after much anguished haggling with the opinionated groups inside the Society, who gave her this guidance. During the height of the digging and paving he seldom arrived home before one o'clock in the morning. He roamed Catacumba's mountainsides, dead tired, mind-weary, but hopeful—marveling at the progress and quietly urging the favelados on.

While Flavio da Silva would be incapable of thinking of himself as a symbol of any sort, thousands of favelados would now live a somewhat better life because he had been plucked from their ranks to dramatize their fate. The truth of this was conveyed in a letter José Gallo wrote to Ruth Fowler some time later:

> The Catacumba project is still most active. I wish you could come to Rio and see, hear, and feel the enthusiasm and happiness in all these men, women, and children who work on the project. Already the favela has twelve main alleys, and several small ones, paved with concrete stairways that could last forever. The favelados themselves have contributed all the labor by sacrificing their Sundays and holidays. The money sent by *Life*'s readers bought 55 tons

of cement, 217 cubic meters of sand, 200 meters of gravel, a ton of steel bars, 600 planks, 200 kilos of nails, and all the tools needed.

"In honor of Flavio we have built a community center and founded a self-help society of 400 people which holds meetings twice a week to discuss local problems and to get to know each other better. We have expanded into social work, hygienic care, sickness prevention, and handicrafts for women. Our work here is now being studied by many observers, students, and others interested in solving problems in the other outlying favelas. Sargent Shriver, of the Peace Corps, has visited Catacumba also. It is a miracle, Ruth. It is wonderful. The favelados wish for me to express their gratitude. . . .

Ten

After nine months at Denver, Flavio was now entering the happiest period of his stay. Between Christmas and March he had been hospitalized only once, and then to have a tooth extracted. His academic record was much improved and he was expected to receive passing marks. He was not yet reading at the top level for his class, but he had volunteered to stay after school to eliminate that weakness. Now that he enjoyed school, he completed his assignments on time and had an excellent attendance record. Most important, he was trying much harder.

At the end of Flavio's first school year, Psychologists at the Institute again tested him. They found that Flavio had special mechanical talent and the temperament to go with it. They recommended that his verbal skills should not be neglected, but that a vocational curriculum would be more realistic for him. They saw no reason why Flavio should not skip at least one grade or perhaps two.

That spring Flavio enjoyed his first Easter egg hunt in the fields surrounding the Gonçalves cabin in the foothills. The night before, Kathy and José had spent an hour hiding the multicolored eggs beneath rocks, crevices, and clumps of weeds. The next morning, after the eggs were found, a race was set up in which each boy used his nose to push the egg to the finish line. Rick, the winner, was rewarded with a sack of chocolate eggs.

Now that school was out, Flavio was free to enjoy even more time with the Gonçalves family, and he stayed long weekends running from Friday to Monday mornings. On the Fourth of July, excitedly awaiting his first parade, he stood on a downtown Denver street with the Gonçalves boys, first hearing the drums, then watching the uniformed band step in rhythm around the corner. When the American flag passed, Flavio, copying Rick and Mark, saluted grandly. Then came the fife, flute, and horn blowers, the mayor, the politicians, the local heroes of recent wars, the weary heroes of ancient wars, the starched-white Daughters of the American Revolution, the bunting-wrapped, blushing girls on red, white, and blue floats, the Boy scouts, the Girl Scouts, the fire brigade, the police brigade, and a block full of nondescript strgglers stepping raggedly to the music. The boys watched until the final note sounded and the last of the marchers disappeared down the street. Then José took them to Kathy's father's cabin in the foothills. There, after stuffing themselves with hot dogs and hamburgers, which Flavio helped cook, the boys bobbed about the lake in the boat they had received at Christmas. Flavio gave everyone a scare by turning over the boat and getting trapped beneath it: Kathy jumped in to pull him out. At sundown they drove to the edge of a nearby canyon to watch the fireworks.

This began a series of weekend summer pleasures with the Gonçalves family that carried over into early autumn. Beside numerous trips to the cabin, they went to movies, county and state fairs, ballgames and picnics, and took scouting and camping trips, short tours along the Colorado River, and a trip to Pueblo. Flavio learned to bait a hook and cast a line; he caught a magnificent trout one Sunday morning but balked when it came time to eat it. He learned to use a bow and arrow with startling accuracy and became able to identify red cedar, blue spruce, chipmunks, rabbits, skunks, red squirrels, deer, frogs, black and yellow leaf beetles, and just about everything in the woods that caught his eye. Lying awake nights he got to know the hoot of the owl, the howl of the coyote, and the sound of crickets rubbing wetness from their wings.

Into the foothills with Flavio and the Gonçalves on an August weekend went Philip Gantevoort, one of Flavio's earliest benefactors, who wrote him frequently and sent him money each month. Philip, a middle-aged man of Dutch ancestry and a former Boy Scout Master in Holland, was now a housekeeper for four priests of a Diocese in Babylon, Long Island. He had arrived in Denver for his first visit with Flavio, bringing him a handsome stamp collection. Philip was only one of many people who continued sending letters and gifts to Flavio. Because of Flavio's inability, Kathy often wrote his replies and had him sign them. The entire group went camping, barbecuing their dinner and toasting marshmallows over night bonfires.

After early mass on Sundays, Flavio helped the boys construct miniature airplane, boat, and automobile models, but Kathy always set aside an hour to tutor him in English and Portuguese. When he showed exceptional progress she rewarded him with candy or something he wanted that she could afford.

During August Kathy eased Flavio into geography. He could draw a map of Colorado and knew that it was bordered by Utah, Wyoming, New Mexico, and chunks of Kansas, Oklahoma, and Nebraska. He was mildly shocked to learn that his own country was officially called The United States of Brazil, and that it covered over three million square miles. He had re-

ally never thought of it extending beyond the city of Rio. Kathy
talked to him about everything from Brazil's government to its
plant life. He knew that Carlos Lacerda was the Governor of
Guanabara State and that the nation's capital was Brasilia.
Through photographs, he could also identify a Brazilian monkey, a jacaranda tree, a pepper tree, guava fruit, a rose-purple
morning glory, and other such things that were indigenous to
his native land. Besides trying in every way possible to keep
Flavio happy during the short time left to him in America,
Kathy was also trying to prepare him for that day when that
time would run out. By summer's end the Gonçalves family
thought of Flavio as their own. For them it had been an enjoyable three months; for him it had been something close to paradise.

At the beginning of Flavio's second year of school, Miriam
Clifford, an examiner for Denver's educational system, gave
Flavio further intelligence tests. She found his interest in
things so intense that it was difficult to shift his attention away
from one material to another. He seemed driven in his search
for correct answers, and she found him even better adjusted
than his report had shown in July. Miriam Clifford doubted,
however, that Flavio could successfully skip a grade. Flavio
had little or no experience with youngsters of his own age, and
she feared that his present association with the younger second
graders might handicap his personality and social development. She recommended that Flavio associate with children of
his own size but in a dormitory setting. If he got along there
with thirteen- and fourteen-year-olds, then he could be placed
in a higher class. In this advanced situation he could be given
work in keeping with his knowledge, and pushed much harder.
As a result of this opinion Flavio was moved once again to
the boys' building with patients his age. Jesse Harrison and
Donna Rust, an older couple, were house parents there, and

they ran a strict house. On week nights everyone was to be in bed by nine o'clock, up at 6:45, and into the meeting room, bright and scrubbed, by 7:30. There, medical appointments and general announcements were made, then breakfast was served at 7:50 sharp. Everyone, with their teeth brushed, was to be off to school by 8:30.

The children came back to the Institute for lunch, then returned to school until 3:20. Recreation lasted until dinner time, which was served at 5:00. After that Jess usually organized a baseball game, which was Flavio's favorite sport, and everyone acknowledged he was very good at it. For a while he had difficulty going to sleep at the prescribed hour; after the lights were out he would "fool around a bit." But some stern persuasion by Jess quickly brought him around. Otherwise Flavio adjusted well to this routine.

Each week the boys were given different chores such as delivering mail or laundry to each section. Flavio performed his duties promptly and willingly, then went off to the study room by 7:00 P.M. for more English and Portuguese lessons with Kathy, who now came in the evenings. He was given catechism lessons each Tuesday, and he attended mass at 7:00 Sunday mornings.

The months of discipline at Cheltenham and the Institute were paying off. Jess and Donna now had good reason to be pleased with Flavio. When he first arrived at Willens Building he would walk off abruptly in the middle of a game or a conversation, leaving the other person to contend with the empty air; now he excused himself. In the early days he would burst into the rooms of the other boys without knocking or excusing himself; now he knocked first, then asked to enter. He no longer picked fights, but fought only to protect himself and what was his, and he fought by the rules. A very small boy who was a kind of pet to everyone walked up to Flavio one morning and bloodied his nose. It was his way of reacting to Flavio's

growing popularity. Flavio simply gave the boy a gentle smack
on the butt and sent him on his way. A year before he would
have forked two fingers into his attacker's eyes and kneed him
in the groin. There was no doubt that Flavio was becoming
another kind of boy. He seemed to have mellowed into his role
as a celebrity. New arrivals sometimes mentioned that they
had seen him in *Life* magazine, and although this pleased him
he never bragged about it. Donna and Jess found him a very af-
fectionate, but one who needed a lot of attention. But they
made it a point never to treat him any differently from the
others.

Flavio suddenly began writing home once a week, but he
seldom talked about his family. And though he used to show
Donna pictures of his brothers and sisters, he was always reluctant, for some reason, to identify them. He never got letters
from home, and no longer complained about it; a year of silence had conditioned him not to expect any. He just didn't
seem to care anymore. Most of the children at the Institute
were usually anxious to go home and could tell you exactly
when they were scheduled to leave. Flavio would never openly
admit it, but he had a way of letting everyone know that he did
not want to go back to Rio. It got so that at the mere mention of
Brazil he would frown, turn, and walk off without saying a
word. Over the summer the attitudes of the other boys toward
him had changed considerably; everybody suddenly liked him.
But he still politely avoided personal attachments or making
close friends; he would remain a loner.

Adeline Kosmata was Flavio's second-year teacher at Cheltenham. After reading his 1961 reports, she feared that he
might possibly fall back into his old behavior patterns and that
he would have lost his sharpness for reading and arithmetic
during the summer vacation. Finding him so nicely adjusted
and responsive to his studies was a pleasant surprise. He now
counted into high numbers, solved simple problems in addi-

tion and subtraction, wrote English fairly well, and in some instances spoke it better than many of his classmates, and without a trace of accent. During that first quarter of 1961 he had been tardy fourteen times; he wasn't tardy once within that same period of 1962. Whereas he had once been easily distracted, bored, and sulky in class, he was now happy, attentive, and good-mannered.

Flavio was still acutely aware of the age difference between himself and his classmates, and this probably hindered his forming close friendships but it didn't affect his overall attitude toward them. Again Flavio developed into the most entertaining story teller in the class, as well as its most skilled dancer. He was becoming more and more skilled with his hands, and Adeline Kosmata began steering him toward vocational interests—partially because she was afraid that too strong an academic program might discourage him. His mid-term report card was a favorable one; a footnote read: "He is like a beautiful moth emerging from a shapeless cocoon. Everyone loves him. Only Flavio could have done it."

Flavio da Silva had, after twenty months, grown to love America. It had given him more than most children around the world ever get—a small fortune, a house for his family, a chance to learn, love, and to live out a full and healthy life. It was a place where he had been close to complete happiness, and he did not want to leave it. His concern about going back to Brazil was growing rapidly into open rebellion. Suddenly he wanted to speak only English, no Portuguese, and he stopped writing to his mother. Then one evening, as José Gonçalves was driving him back to the Institute, Flavio declared outright that he never wanted to go back to Brazil.

"Why?" José asked.

"Because people in Brazil were mean to me. Here they treat

me very good. That's why I don't want to go back. Do you understand?"

"How were they mean to you?"

"They tried to beat us with sticks when they heard we were getting out of the favela. They threw rocks at us and spit on us. My poor mother had to carry around a broomstick to protect us sometimes."

"But things will be different now. Your family has a nice new house. And they have food and clothes now."

"You don't understand. Those people there are mean. They don't care about me like people do here." Although José tried, no amount of cajoling could turn Flavio's heart toward Brazil.

The next day Kathy spoke to him. "You will have to go back to Brazil, Flavio. There is nothing any of us can do about that. It is the law. And it will be a shame if you don't learn to speak better Portuguese. What about your family? Have you forgotten them?"

"I have not forgotten them. They have forgotten me. I send them letters and presents. And do they answer me ever? No. No, I want never to go back there. I will do all I can to stay in America. Here I have a chance."

Kathy Gonçalves, nevertheless, continued to talk to him in Portuguese, although he would answer her in English. When word reached him that his mother had given birth to another girl he only shrugged. "What is her name?" he asked. When he was told that it was Rute he smiled, knowing it had been named for Ruth Fowler. "Rute," he said, "is a very pretty name for a girl."

"Wouldn't you like to see her?"

He scratched his head, thought for a moment, then answered, "Yes, but not right away."

During Flavio's sojourn in Denver, perhaps no one was closer to him or knew him better than Kathy Gonçalves. Her devotion to his welfare was almost fierce, and it was probably this devotion that generated the difficulties that arose between her and the Institute. The trouble grew out of Flavio's longing to stay in America; for now, in desperation, he had turned to Kathy for help. She knew that what he wanted was impossible, but she couldn't help but sympathize with him.

It was hard for her to keep telling him what he hated most to hear—that he would have to go back to Brazil. Even if no one else in America demanded it, the immigration authorities would, and so would his father. Despite this Kathy gradually allowed her feelings to put her at odds with the realities of Flavio's situation. Time was closing in on him; there was less than six months left. So now, with the same furious zeal with which she had set out to educate him, she got deeply involved in the Institute's plans for his departure and future education.

Dr. Samuel Bukantz's assistant, Evelyn Beimers, remembers that "We got a little concerned when she suddenly began to call us so often. She was a nice, warm lady and was probably hoping against hope that the Institute might find some way to keep him longer. She seemed confused, frustrated, and *over involved,* perhaps because of her love for him and her desire to help him. I don't remember what it was exactly all about, but there was a pretty warm confrontation between her and Flavio's house parents. And I think that they told her pretty bluntly that they were responsible for him, not her." Nothing could have hurt Kathy Gonçalves more. She registered her feelings in a letter to Dr. Bukantz, the Institute's Director, and hand delivered it to his office that same Monday evening.

The following morning, during a meeting to which Kathy had been summoned to explain her position, Dr. Bukantz listened rather impatiently, softly drumming his fingers on his desk. There were a few moments of silence after she finished. Then, with what Kathy termed "cold officiousness," the doctor turned to her and said, "I am afraid you are making independent judgments beyond your authority. The Institute cannot tolerate this, since we are solely responsible for his welfare. Certainly we do appreciate what you have done for Flavio and the love and concern you have shown him. But we have a strong desire here at the Institute to coordinate our activities so that the program of his medical and psychological care remains a staff function and not an individual one."

Kathy returned home frustrated and angry with the doctor's rebuff, feeling that she had been undeservedly censured. Her response was defined in a note from Evelyn Beimers to Dr. Bukantz. It read:

> "Mrs. Gonçalves called the office this morning. She was very upset and crying, saying she would not be at the Institute today. I got the impression that she would not be coming at all, not only this week but from now on."

Overnight the situation had become irreconcilable. Kathy remembered the call to Evelyn Beimers. "I was very upset, extremely upset," she said. "It had all happened over such a small thing. I don't even remember what it was about, and I was astonished that it reached such large proportions. Dr. Bukantz was very surprised when I came back that following Friday. He must have thought that I wouldn't because my next check had a note in it saying it would be my last one.

"Flavio hated so much the thought of going home. All of his memories of the past were so negative. And I hated to see him go. But I told him that he was prepared now to become a good Brazilian. He never understood this. He just kept saying, 'I don't want to go back to live with my father.' Poor Flav. I felt so sorry for him. Here he was trying to bear the huge responsibility of being a symbol, when he couldn't even realize what he was meant to symbolize. He was like a son, and I would have taught him forever. I will never understand why the hospital terminated my services."

The following week Silva Najberg, a seventeen-year-old girl from Rio de Janeiro, was assigned to Flavio as his Portuguese language instructor. Being fired as Flavio's tutor proved a traumatic experience for Kathy. "I wasn't terribly surprised. I had vibrations, a feeling that something I didn't know about was going on. The only thing I can think of is that I was bucking the system somehow. But Flavio meant more to me than just a job. When I got the impression that I wasn't to see him any more I protested vehemently, and I said to them, 'Now wait a minute, you don't have to pay me. I'll be there anyway.' I might be able to understand why I was dismissed but he wouldn't, and I didn't want him to think that I was no longer his friend. But they allowed me to continue seeing him and tutoring him informally. I don't think they cared, as long as I didn't rock the boat."

Dr. Bukantz was distressed by the rift. While he could have prevented Kathy from taking Flavio home as usual on the weekends, he chose not to do so. Fortunately, Flavio was never aware of the fighting over him.

In fact, things continued pretty much the same between Flavio and the Gonçalves family. Kathy continued to pick him up on either Friday evenings or Saturday mornings. But now she crammed his weekends with harder work and less play. The little time left for him would be used to the greatest advantage. Staying up with him after Rick, Mark, and Neil had gone to bed, she often worked with him late into the night.

"You're going to make a good Brazilian citizen, but you're going to have to work hard at it," she would tell him repeatedly. "You can't wind up in the favela again. That would be a tragedy." Flavio must have understood; the more she pushed him the harder he tried.

During the twelve years Flavio had spent on Catacumba,

no one ever bothered to remind him of his birthday, and for some reason he had not bothered to ask what date it fell upon. His mother, Nair, had long kept the recorded date on a soiled grocery sack beneath the mattress. So April 14, 1963 proved to be a big day for Flavio. Donna Rust and Jesse Harrison had a party for him and served cookies, lemonade, and ice cream. The boys at the dormitory sang "Happy Birthday" to him. A few gave him presents, but a drawing by Mitsu, one of several boys invited from Willens Building, was the highlight of the party. It depicted a scowling Flavio with devil's horns protruding from his head, arriving with his bags at Willens Building. Juxtaposed with that image was another one of a happy, smiling Flavio. A halo had replaced the horns and Flavio had sprouted a set of angel's wings. Mitsu was getting a message across in a not-so-subtle way, and Flavio received it.

Flavio's class at Cheltenham wrote a poem to him on a large sheet of drawing paper, using colored crayons, and hung it on the wall near his seat. He had not noticed it when he first entered the room. The entire class had awed him by serenading him with the "Happy Birthday" song again. Then, with a big grin, he discovered the poem. It read:

> Dear Flavio you make us all so happy
> With all your dancing and tales and stuff.
> You keep us laughing all the time
> But we don't get enough.
> So believe us all when we say
> We wish dear Flavio a happy birthday.

In appreciation Flavio put on a five-minute exhibition of the samba. Then he instantly invented and told a tale about a nice, big, cheerful hot dog, so big it had to be hauled to town on a trailer truck. "But when that cheerful hot dog found out that those greedy people were getting ready to eat him, he got so mad he exploded and blew up the whole town. After that those greedy people wouldn't try to eat up no more cheerful hot dogs, because there wasn't enough left of those people to make even a teeny weeny hamburger. So let that be a lesson to all greedy people who like to eat big, cheerful hot dogs!"

The third and final party took place at the Gonçalves house that night. There were more gifts, a pair of blue jeans, a sweater, a pen and pencil set, plus a birthday cake with fourteen candles—one for each year of his life. Greeting cards and money had come from Phil Gantevoort, from an elderly woman by the name of Irene Tatum who lived in Schenectady, New York, and from others in different parts of the country. Flavio thought that his brothers and sisters would like seeing all these wonderful birthday cards; so he decided to save them. He tried putting them in his clothes drawer but there were just too many. Finally he stuffed them into a couple of shoe boxes that Kathy gave him, and secured the boxes with a rope.

The celebration momentarily eased the dread of his impending departure, but shortly after Flavio started working on anyone who he thought might help him avert that departure—the doctors, nurses, house parents, the Gonçalves, and even some of his dormitory mates. But it was all to no avail. Dr. Bukantz had already written Ruth Fowler asking her to start making definite plans for his leaving, and for a month José Gallo had gone from one São Paulo boarding school to another, trying to get one of them to accept Flavio for the following year. Rio, with the pressures and involvement in his family, might make his transition much harder. São Paulo was at a reasonable distance yet was not so far away as to prevent his coming home on some weekends or holidays. The American School at São Paulo would have been ideal for Flavio; for there he could have continued with his English. They ac-

cepted him at first, then abruptly rejected him on the grounds
that the publicity he had received might hurt his relationships
with the other students. Twenty other Brazilian schools refused him for the same reason or for reasons even more ob-
scure. With some difficulty José finally convinced a Protestant
boarding school to take him. The fund of $10,000 set aside for
him was virtually untouched. In Brazil this would be enough
to finance his schooling and start him out in life. He would get
the balance of money when he became twenty-one years of
age.

Because of Flavio's imminent discharge and the need to
plan his future education, it was time to sum up his potential
and to measure the changes he had undergone in two years.
All his previous tests had been consistently termed unsuc-
cessful, but since they were biased in favor of American
middle-class children, it was quite possible that they didn't
accurately reflect the true learning ability of someone from
Flavio's background.

Mindful of this, and having heard so much about Flavio's
innate brightness, Dr. Jonathan Weiss, one of the Institute's
finest psychologists, gave him a non-verbal test that didn't
require any prior cultural learning. The IQ derived was a
shockingly low 61 (average intelligence is scored at 100). Simi-
larly, Flavio's drawings of the human figure revealed a primi-
tive, childish quality in keeping with the results of his former
tests. Weiss found it hard to believe what he had found. He
could only conclude that "Flavio simply appeared to be
brighter." An examination of his test behavior left little doubt
that his old scores were indeed accurate and that what had
caused the oft-expressed doubts as to their correctness was
Flavio's social skill and charm, plus his eagerness to learn. It
was these attributes that lent him that air of brightness.

Weiss further described Flavio as a child with a limited

ability for abstract thinking, but, on the other hand, quite adaquate for doing things where requirements were very simple. He was also against pushing Flavio toward intellectual skills, and advised manual training in some area that might interest him.

The Institute had lived up to its promise and saved Flavio, but its doctors were still uncertain about what might happen to him back in Brazil. They could only speculate on why he had suffered so few attacks while he was in the Institute. Perhaps the pollen count was greater in Brazil than it was in Colorado; still, this might not have been the factor. Dr. Fallier's team had investigated every issue thoroughly; yet Flavio's case would remain a mystery to them. Many acute asthmatics present baffling problems: some children at the Institute claimed their attacks were aggravated by pleasant as well as unpleasant emotions. One boy said that his attacks came not only when he was tense or fearful of something, but also when he was laughing at Bob Hope on television. This seemed to suggest that any kind of intense emotion could trigger an attack.

Flavio's sudden change had been dramatic and rewarding, but it was difficult to thoroughly understand the reasons for his recovery. Asthma brought him to Denver; so one might assume that when he returned to Brazil he might welcome an attack to bring him back—and certainly this was a possibility. Some children returned home in excellent condition, then became worse than they had been before coming to the Institute. Others held on to the gains they made. Some children claimed they could induce asthma attacks whenever they wanted to, something that was hard to test. The doctors couldn't just say, "All right, prove it." There were also children who said they could bring on attacks at home but not at the Institute, although there was no such talk from Flavio. Only through constant re-evaluation in the control labs could the doctors hope to learn just how much a child might influence his illness.

Flavio would spend his last Thanksgiving in America with the Gonçalves family, and it was natural too that Kathy would try to make it memorable for him. She and José had shopped a good part of the previous afternoon for the biggest turkey they could find; it had to feed thirteen. Kathy had invited her parents and her cousin, Jack. He and his wife and three children, Johnny, Susie, and Stacey had driven up from Texas for the occasion. Even with the extra leaves the regular table wasn't big enough, but somehow they would all squeeze in. It was covered with Kathy's finest lace tablecloth and set with her best silverware. While she put the final touches on the dinner, Flavio and the other children worked up appetites in a furious game of hide and seek.

José bragged that Kathy had never roasted a turkey so well, made tastier trimmings, or baked such delicious apple and pumpkin pies. Flavio was given a huge drumstick; he also got the wishbone. And when he and Rick broke it into two pieces, Flavio got the smaller end, thereby losing his chance to make a wish. Rick graciously offered to trade ends but Flavio refused. "It won't work," he said. "I wouldn't get my wish anyhow." No one needed to ask him what his wish might have been. After dinner Flavio volunteered to entertain five-year-old Stacey. She was almost as big as he was, but he lugged her around the house on his shoulder and bounced her on his knee in much the same way he used to bounce Zacarias. Because it was Thanksgiving, Kathy spared him his usual evening lessons. Furthermore, it was too noisy and she was worn out. She did however spend a few minutes explaining the origin of Thanksgiving to him.

As Flavio's time at the Institute dwindled, so did that of some of the other children. It was a bright spring day when

Mitsu left for good. Flavio went over to Willens and helped him carry his bags to his parents' car. In parting the two shook hands and wished each other good luck. Afterward, Flavio grew pensive, thinking perhaps that his time wasn't far off. "I guess Mitsu won't ever be coming back," he said to Donna Rust.

"We hope not, Flavio," Donna had answered.

Flavio's brow wrinkled. "Don't you ever want to see him again?"

"Yes, of course, but not as a patient."

Flavio thought for a moment. "I see. He was a crazy little guy but I don't like to see him go."

"Well, he will be much happier at home with his brothers and sisters."

"Why do you say that?"

"They are his family. He loves them and they love him. They will be glad to have him home again."

"I love my brothers and sisters too," he answered, "but I won't be happy when I go back. It will be bad there."

"It will be different this time, Flavio."

"No, it won't be no different. My father, he will be the same. Those bad people in Brazil will be the same. I don't ever want to go back there." No amount of persuasion from Donna could make him feel otherwise.

The sight of a child suffering a severe asthma attack can be terrifying, especially when it happens in the middle of the night, miles from a doctor. In the agony of trying to breathe, a child's heart pounds, the veins throb, the throat swells, sweat pours, and the eyes bulge; and there is always an awful choking when mucus begins clogging the airways. Because many parents panic when such an attack comes, the Institute invited them to visit near the end of their child's stay to instruct them in ways to cope with such an emergency. They were warned *not* to panic but to call a doctor immediately, because once the lungs filled with mucus it sometimes took six hours before the drugs took full effect, and then it might be too late. They were told that inadequate treatment (too late or too little) could also be fatal. They were cautioned that overtreatment with adrenalin nebulizers could cause lung destruction or overload the heart and that mouth-to-mouth resuscitation might, as a last resort, prevent their child from dying en route to the hospital. If there were dietary problems, the parents were alerted to them and asked to ease any emotional strains at home that might aggravate their child's condition.

Flavio had no parents around to advise; so during his final months he was brought in more often for checkups and encouraged to ask questions about his diet and the medicines he had taken. He was also taught how to aid himself in case he became ill on a plane or back in Brazil. There had been relatively few deaths at the hospital over the years from heart failures and infections; those who died had been brought to the Institute too late for the doctors to reverse the ravages of the disease. One boy rode his bicycle off the premises and was killed by a car. But the overall mortality rate at the Institute was remarkably low.

Finally resigned to leaving, Flavio began making plans for his departure. He sent all of his clothes out to be cleaned, wrote farewells to his American friends, and collected items and gifts he had treasured to take home to his family. Phil Gantevoort sent him $200 for new clothes as a going-away present. Kathy spent a whole Saturday with Flavio shopping at the downtown Denver stores. Despite his gloom about leaving, Flavio had a lot to be thankful for. In two years he had changed from a frail, sickly slum kid into a growing, healthy boy. During the final twelve months, he had not suffered one serious attack despite one of Colorado's worst winters in fifty years. He seemed only to have needed good medical care, wholesome food, dry mountain air, and clean, sympathetic surroundings. He was growing much faster now than other boys who were also small for their age; it was as if his body realized it had a lot of catching up to do. He was now 7½ inches taller and 22¼ pounds heavier than when he arrived.

It hadn't been easy; he had made great progress, due a lot to his own courageous spirit. He still had a lot to make up in other areas; yet he had learned good manners, respect for privacy, and sportsmanship. His biggest triumph had been learning to respect the property of others. Extremely generous with his own valuables, he had assumed, back in those angry days at Willens Building, that others would also be generous. As his days grew shorter his circle of friends widened. His comrades, in fairness and in their own concept of justice, could not accuse him of not giving as much as he had taken.

But the truth was inescapable: we had dreams for Flavio da Silva that were hopelessly beyond his reach. It was as if we expected abundant fruit from a sapling already gone barren. Those working with him had searched hard for some way to push him to the level of children of his own age, but it had been fruitless. Flavio was always being described as charming, bright, and very endearing, with leadership qualities. He *was* a leader, but with children much younger than himself. His marks in school were good, but in a grade substantially below that of a child his age. Fate had deprived Flavio of simple things like reading, writing, and adequate nutrition for too long. At twelve, age had already become a negative factor.

There is a readiness for learning, a peak for acquiring academic skills. Flavio was past that peak when he arrived at Denver. And although his performances had improved over the two years, there was no spectacular change in relation to his age group. He had taken a big leap into social middle-class America, and done a good job. His English was now better than his Portuguese. But he would be going back to something radically different from either the favela or Denver. And although his Portuguese was very much improved, he would not be able to complete scholastically with the average Brazilian boy of his age. Despite all of his admirable qualities, Flavio da Silva's future remained unpromising. The early corrosive illness, along with the ruinous deprivation, had already taken its toll. Yet one could not disassociate his positive qualities from the negative. The major problem was that Flavio was below average, a problem that many at the Institute, having been caught up in his charm and social amenities, were reluctant to accept.

At last there was only a week left for Flavio, a day, then the final hour, when, on July 27, 1963, he was officially discharged from the Institute. Ruth Fowler and Virginia Hansen, the principal at Cheltenham who first helped Flavio with his English, would accompany him to New York by train. He would spend a day in New York with me, then fly on to Brazil with Virginia.

During his last moments at the Institute Flavio sat alone in his room with tears welling in his eyes, feeling abandoned by all those who had befriended him for so long. When Donna Rust found him there staring out the window, he jumped up and wiped away the tears. Then, smiling, he said, "Okay, let's go." His bags, crammed with gifts, new clothes, books, records, and some stones he had collected during his outings in the foothills, were much heavier than when he had arrived two years before. Almost silently Jess Harrison and Donna, along with a small group of boys, helped him with his belongings to the car that waited with Ruth Fowler and Virginia Hansen. At last he stood with a half-grin on his face, dressed in a natty checkered summer jacket and dark-blue slacks, waving goodbye to everyone. Then before entering the car he took some marbles from his pocket and gave them to the boys who had come to see him off. Sadness was all over his face as he left these friends and the home he had come to love. He was still waving as the car pulled off, but before it hit the outer road he had fallen into a morose silence.

The Gonçalves family, along with Kathy's father and mother, went to Denver's Union Station to see Flavio off. Everybody was dressed in their Sunday best, for this was a very special occasion. By the time they were all gathered, departure time was near. José hustled about snapping pictures of the group lined up beside the sleek streamliner that would take Flavio on the first leg of his journey homeward. The farewells were hurried but warm, a bit nervous but free of emotionalism. Promises were made—everyone would write Flavio and he in turn would write to everyone. At the last moment, José lined up his family and himself beside Flavio, and Ruth took their picture—all smiling radiantly into the camera. The conductor shouted "All aboard!" Flavio kissed Kathy and shook hands with all the others. He paused on the train steps for a moment so that José could take one last photograph; then he waved and hurried to the window beside his seat. He was still waving furiously to the boys as the train began rolling out of the station. As the train rumbled further into the distance, Kathy Gonçalves stood for a long moment watching it. "Well, kids, Flav is gone," she said. Then she turned and they went home.

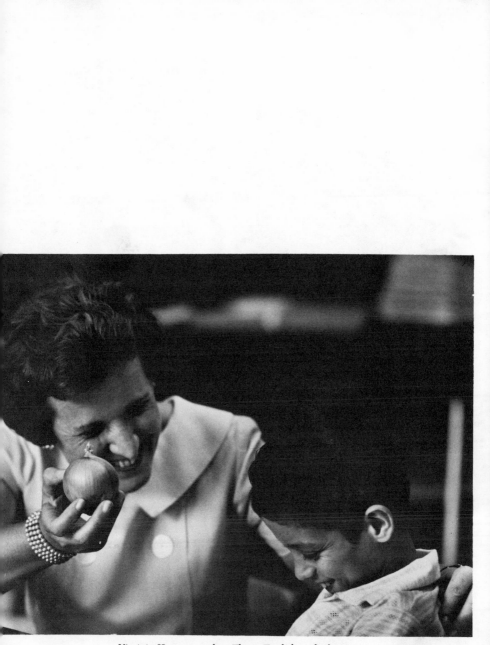

Virginia Hansen teaches Flavio English with the
aid of an onion, Denver, 1961. (*Carl Iwasaki*)

Kathy Gonçalves and Flavio in the Denver hills, 1961. (*José Gonçalves*)

Flavio catches his first fish, Denver, 1961. (*José Gonçalves*)

Flavio with the three Gonçalves boys. From left to right, Neil, Mark, and Rick. (*José Gonçalves*)

Flavio and the Gonçalves boys July 27, 1963, just before he takes train for New York. (*José Gonçalves*)

Flavio and Mark Gonçalves, spring 1962, Denver, Colorado. (*José Gonçalves*)

Christmas at the Gonçalves home, 1963. (*José Gonçalves*)

Flavio's birthday cake, April 14, 1963. (*José Gonçalves*)

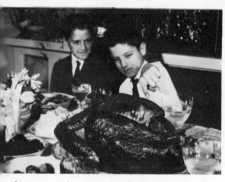

anksgiving at the Gonçalves home. Flavio's very st turkey dinner. (*José Gonçalves*)

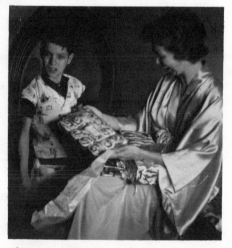

Christmas, 1961. Flavio presents Kathy sweet rolls for a present. (*José Gonçalves*)

Flavio at bat during summer vacation trip with the Gonçalves family, Denver, 1962. (*José Gonçalves*)

**PHOTOGRAPHS
FROM JOSÉ GONÇALVES'
SCRAPBOOK**

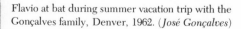

Flavio waves goodbye to the Gonçalves family from the train that
will take him to New York. (*José Gonçalves*)

Eleven

"Well, you could say we have finally broken his cycle of fear, that vicious cycle that sometimes sends patients back to us in worse condition than they were when they left. Now he is older, more mature, more confident. The panic is gone; he has learned to live comfortably with the disease. Yet, who knows, if he should ever be sent back to the favela things might change overnight. Then all we have done may not matter. The attacks, the suffering and despair they bring, could start all over again."

CONSTANTINE FALLIERS, M.D.

July 27, 1963

Flavio was scheduled to stay in New York for forty-eight hours before flying on to Brazil. This would give the two of us approximately twelve of those hours to spend together. Ex-

145

tremely anxious to see him once again and to rekindle our friendship, I had flown from Paris for the meeting. After I left Flavio in Denver, *Life* assignments sent me around most of the world. During these long journeys I thought of him very often and with the good feeling that he was being given the best possible care. It was exhilarating to find that people in such places as England, France, Spain, Italy, and Germany were still concerned about his welfare. It was always the same.

> *"Comment va votre ami, Flavio?"*
> *"Como esta su amigo, Flavio?"*
> *"Wie gehts, Flavio?"*
> *"Come sta il tuo amico, Flavio?"*

I could always reply that he was coming along just fine; the Institute at Denver had been a godsend. Nevertheless, I felt guilty for not having given him more personal attention while he was there. I had made plans to spend his second Christmas in Denver with him, but at the last moment I had been given another assignment abroad. Now, with his arrival, my conscience goaded me. It would be impossible to do in twelve hours what could have been more effectively done during those last 720 days. So I rationalized my shortcomings and took refuge in my nobler intentions. Our reunion would take care of itself, and I felt that it would be a very special one.

Flavio was sharing a suite with Virginia Hansen at the same hotel he had stayed on his initial stop over in New York. My anxiety grew as the elevator stopped at his floor. When I knocked at the door it practically flew open. And there, with a big smile on his face, was Flavio.

"Gordon!" he shouted.

We threw our arms about each other; then he took my hand and led me into the room where Ruth Fowler and her assistant, Vivi Stiles, were waiting. Virginia had gone for her passport. It was a wonderful moment for all of us. There were so many things I wanted to ask him and tell him. I asked him how he was and he told me he was fine, and he looked fine in his natty summer outfit. The once pallid face was now tanned and he was taller and heavier than I had expected him to be—even after two years at the Institute. It was hard to remember that this smiling, handsome, and apparently healthy boy was the same sickly, frightened, and insecure twelve-year-old I had left in Denver twenty-four months before.

"I am so glad to see you," Flavio said. "What are we going to do today?" He was buttoning his jacket and adjusting his tie, already preparing himself to go.

"We will see New York, eat, see New York and eat," I answered. And, truly impressed, I added, "You are speaking very good English."

"Oh yes, I speak very good English now. I learned it very fast, very fast," he said proudly.

"And how is your Portuguese?" Ruth asked.

"Oh that," he said with an impish grin, "that is coming along just so-so. I like to speak English much better. I don't want to talk about Portuguese." He tugged at my arm. "Come on, let's go see New York. Okay, Gordon?" We said goodbye to Ruth and Vivi and took off.

It was a lovely summer day and fittingly brilliant, with shafts of sunlight knifing down between the tall buildings along Fifth Avenue as we walked. "This is better than Christmas," Flavio said. "Everything is so pretty." It was his first chance to see the city in the way he was seeing it now; that sudden attack of nerves and vomiting had kept him indoors on his first visit.

I already knew that Flavio longed to stay in America and that he loathed going back to Brazil. But I hoped that by now he had accepted the inevitable and that our brief reunion would be spared any agonizing on his part. I believe he sensed this, for we started off happily, as though some tacit agreement lay between us to avoid the dismal thought of his approaching departure. With nothing definite in mind we just drifted, he with his hand in mine, pulling me toward everything that interested him—a burly man dressing a bare store window mannequin; a display of six television sets tuned to six different stations ("Boy, I'd like to have all those in my room and turn them all on at once. You could watch football and a movie, and baseball at the same time!"); another window full of live puppies for sale, a large rubber elephant that looked real, advertising a jungle book; a street vendor wearing a straw hat with small American flags stuck in the band, hawking his wares.

"Look at those crazy doughnuts," Flavio said.

"Those are bagels, idiot, not doughnuts."

"What's a bagel?"

"A Yiddish hard roll."

"What's Yiddish?"

"Are you putting me on, Flavio da Silva?"

"Nope."

"Okay, it's a Jewish language."

"They make hard rolls out of Jewish language?"

He *was* putting me on. There was a grin on his face as wide as a platter. He still had a sense of humor. I had planned on a good lunch in a good restaurant, but Flavio wanted hot dogs, a coke, and ice cream. He won. We ate, then went to the top of the Empire State Building. Flavio enjoyed it all but he liked the elevator ride more than he did the magnificent view of Manhattan. At his insistence we took that interminable ride up and down at least three times.

We spent the rest of the afternoon buying gifts for everyone in his family, even the new baby he hadn't seen. He was painstakingly thoughtful about what his brothers and sisters might like most, remembering the difference two years would make in their individual tastes—"Maria is too big for a doll now. Mario is big enough for a scout knife. Luzia would like a pretty mirror to pretty-up with, and maybe a fancy comb." He wanted only three things for himself: a wrist watch, as many Chubby Checker albums as I was willing to buy, and a portable typewriter. He had never been on a subway, so we took a short ride across town in a cab, then took a subway up to the Time-Life Building. Clark Gable's sudden arrival there couldn't have caused greater commotion than did Flavio's presence in the building. Everyone, in every office, stopped work to get a peek at him. I took him through the *Life* laboratory, and there I arranged for him to watch a darkroom technician make a large blowup. As he watched the image take shape in the developing tray he began to giggle; he could see now that it was a picture of himself. Now he insisted on trying it. "Not this time, old boy," I said, and began to usher him out.

Suddenly he turned to the technician. "Hey, do you think I could get a job in here some day?" he asked him. The technician laughed.

"He's dead serious," I said. And indeed Flavio was. He bent my ear about it the rest of the afternoon.

It was dusk before we returned to the hotel laden down with packages. Virginia was back, and she was helping Vivi and Ruth rearrange Flavio's clothing in his bags. "Well, how did the day go, Flavio?" she asked.

"Huh?" Flavio answered dazedly. Something was wrong. "I forgot something, Gordon! Come, we must go downstairs!" He dropped the packages and pulled me back to the elevator, and we went down to the lobby. There, we made a formidable purchase of bubble gum and candy bars.

Our day had gone as it should have gone, filled with hot dogs, sightseeing, shopping, and fun. There were moments, however, when my thoughts shifted back to Flavio's days and nights on Catacumba; to the forlorn voice of the clinic doctor who had already given up on him; to that day when he got his first pair of shoes, a good meal, and his first real tub bath. Now, as the elevator took us up again, it all seemed so long ago, so impossible even to imagine the incredible distance Flavio had traveled from that pitiful Brazilian shack to this luxurious American hotel. In another few hours he would return to Brazil and to a new starting point, no longer shadowed by deprivation and early death. How, I wondered, would he meet the new challenges awaiting him there? Would the dreaded asthma attacks reoccur? There were so many things to ponder and he seemed so innocently unaware of any of them—his whole attention was on unwrapping a stick of bubble gum.

Our parting moments were spent in the privacy of Flavio's bedroom. "There is something very important I want to ask you," he said, closing the door so that no one outside could hear. "I don't want to go back to Brazil, Gordon. Can't you keep me here like I'm your son?" His voice rose just above a whisper.

"I'm sure your father wouldn't allow it, Flav," I answered. "I asked him about this when you left Rio that night, about adopting you, and he said no. Your family will be anxious to see you. They are all expecting you. After that you will be going to a nice school in São Paulo."

"But I would rather stay here with you. Don't you want me?"

"I sure would. And so would my children, but it is impossible right now, Flav. Maybe . . ." I stopped there, looking beyond his haunting eyes, preferring not to promise him anything that might prove impossible to fulfill.

He sighed. I had been his very last hope, and now I had failed him. After a short silence he said, "Oh, it's not that I don't want to see my family. I love them, but I also love it here in America. I can do so much better here around all my friends, and some day I can send for my family. Don't you see?"

"I understand, Flav, but all those friends you made in

Denver won't be around you. They will be going to their homes in different parts of the country as soon as they are well enough."

We sat again in silence for a few moments until he asked, "Will you help me come back someday?"

"We'll see, Flav. We'll see," I answered. "Things will be much better for you there now."

"You really think so?"

"I know so. Just give it a chance and you will see that I am right." I rose to leave.

"I will try," he promised, and shook my hand as if to seal a bargain.

We went out to join Ruth and Virginia, who were still packing Flavio's recent acquisitions. I helped squeeze a few things into a bag, and explained Flavio's day in New York. Then it was time for me to go. Flavio made me promise that I would come to see him soon. And since there was a possibility that I might fulfill such a promise, I made it. "Try hard in school," I said leaving. He was by now unwrapping a Chubby Checker album.

"I will! I will! You will see!"

We shook hands and embraced once again, and I left hoping that he would try hard. He would be entering another strange school, in another strange place where rewards would be rare and far off. Perhaps his family would help. Perhaps it could give him some love and attention now that it had been relieved of the intolerable stress and misery of poverty. That night Flavio and Virginia took the overnight flight to Brazil.

José Gallo had asked that they avoid Rio and land in Brasilia to forestall any publicity hoopla that might mar Flavio's homecoming. Feeling that this was logical planning, Virginia agreed. But the strategy failed. Immediately after they cleared Brazilian customs they were startled by flashing bulbs of news cameramen.

"José was obviously irritated," Virginia recalled. He rushed us through a side door and whisked us off to a waiting car. It was all so furtive, almost clandestine. In a few moments we were bolting down the highway at a frightening speed. We didn't talk much during the ride into São Paulo. Flavio slept most of the way; he was so tired after the long flight. And what José had to say was somewhat less than polite. He complained that some of the Americans had done more harm than good by spoiling Flavio. He hoped that no one from the States would write him, and that Flavio would forget his whole experience there. I wasn't in a good position, or mood, to argue this point so I refrained from saying much. His attitude toward me wasn't what I would have expected. I felt awkward and unwanted. José's feisty behavior upset me. By the time we reached São Paulo, I was fighting some strange and unwarranted guilt. José kept wondering how the press had found out about our coming to Brasilia. But it was over, and I was no longer concerned."

José and Virginia spent the next day in São Paulo getting Flavio enrolled in school. He would spend the weekend with his family in Rio, then report back for class the following Monday. The school consisted of five one-storey stucco buildings which sat on five acres of land in the northeast section of São Paulo; it was surrounded by lush plant life, pepper and palmetto trees. There were about three hundred students enrolled there, mostly from middle-class Brazilian families; two-thirds of them were boys. The ages of the students ranged from ten to sixteen. Flavio would be placed in the third grade, on a trial basis. He would live in the dormitory room with three other boys, all of them somewhat younger than he, but very close to his size. Unlike at the Institute, there would be no house parents but instead various teachers who lived on the campus would act as counselors. Flavio met the vice-director, a Reverend Moyses Bastos, who showed him the classrooms and the dormitory quarters. Virginia and José walked closely be-

hind Flavio as the director explained what was expected of him
at the school—hard work, good manners, obedience, and the
worship of God. "If you obey those rules you will get along well
here, my son," the director had said at the end of the brief
visit.

Virginia's feelings about their drive to Rio were equally
cheerless. "Perhaps Flavio was unhappy with what he saw at
the school, but I suspected José had said something to him during the night that had turned him against me. In any case he
was almost nonverbal during the trip to Rio, which was a full
day's ride. I tried to talk with him but he clammed up completely. I finally gave up and slept my way into the city."

The reunion was chaotic. Flavio had insisted on wearing his
new American sports jacket and snap-brim hat. He wanted so
much to appear neat when he arrived, and to exemplify the
true American look. Flavio got out of the car with a curious
half-smile on his face and a bag full of presents under his arm.
Mario spotted him first. "It's Flavio!" he shouted back through
the door. By now he was as tall as Flavio, who was waving and
smiling as all his sisters and brothers burst from the house and
ran toward him. He was big, famous brother returning home,
being swept along now through the front yard and onto the
porch. When Nair appeared in the doorway, Flavio broke loose
and warmly embraced her and kissed her cheek. Then his father came out, chewing on a sausage. As they shook hands José
da Silva seemed more interested in his son's appearance than
he was in their greeting. A slight smile creased his face as he
eyed the handsome jacket. Nair seemed stunned, saying
hardly a word; a thankful look was on her face, and a tear hung
from her eye.

Flavio insisted on opening the gifts on the front porch before
entering the house. There was absolute bedlam as he cheerfully doled them out. "Where are my two new sisters?" he
shouted above the din. "Show them to me! I want to see

them!" Little Rute was already standing wide-eyed by his side, agog at the commotion.

Maria lifted her up. "Here, she's right beside you. The other one is asleep." Flavio kissed Rute and dug into the bag for her present and gave it to her. Luzia was already admiring herself in her new mirror as she fluffed out her hair with the comb he had brought her. Mario was off to the side pulling at the blades of his Boy Scout knife. Maria was trying to undo the clasp on her necklace; Batista couldn't make head or tail of the picture puzzle he had spilled out on the porch floor. So it went until everyone had opened their packages and examined their gifts. Nair was quite pleased with her gingham apron, but one distressing moment came when Flavio gave his father a phonograph record. José had looked at it curiously and remarked, "But I don't have anything to play it on."

Flavio stiffened when he entered the house. He stood in the center of the living room and slowly looked around. The neatly furnished home he had remembered from two years before was now a shambles. Then, turning to José Gallo, he said, "This place is a mess." The walls were dirty, the furniture badly scratched and broken, the plastic flowers and all the homey touches the neighbors had added when the family moved in were gone. Flavio moved into the kitchen. Something was boiling on the stove, so at least the stove was working. But the door to the refrigerator had come off, and there was an odor of stale food. The radio was smashed. The faucets had broken and were stopped up with corks; if you uncorked them water jetted out. While the rest of his family examined their presents on the porch Flavio turned to Virginia and then to José Gallo, his arms spread in disgust. "They have wrecked the place," he said unhappily. "Everything is broken and nothing is repaired." One could see now from the clothes lying all over that the nice little bungalow was hopelessly crowded; it was also filthy. No attempt had been made to make Flavio's homecoming a happy one; there wasn't even a place for him to sleep. Eventually he piled some blankets in a corner and lay awake on them most of that night, hoping that the weekend would be quickly over.

On Sunday morning he gathered his older brothers and sisters and scolded them about the condition of the house. "It is like pigs are living here. All of you, how can you not want to live in a clean place? Our poor mother is almost dead from watching after all of you, and you do nothing to help her. Your father is the same. He is making very little, as usual, telling me his truck is always breaking down. Do you want your mother to die from working so hard for you? Please, all of you, promise me you will do better while I am away this time. Maria, you, Mario, and Luzia and Batista are all big enough to help. I want promises from you." With their new gifts in hand, they found it easy to at least promise, and they did.

This pleased Flavio and later that afternoon he sat them down again and spent two spell-binding hours telling them of the beauty and wonders of America, of how he wished to go back one day, make his fortune, and send for all of them. Flavio's dreams were still alive. Just before he left for São Paulo the next morning, Maria had lifted his spirits somewhat. "Hey, Flav," she had said shyly, "you are sure good looking now." Flavio gently touched her arm and smiled his thanks.

Virginia Hansen recalled that after that weekend at home Flavio was in a catatonic state, practically in shock. "On the way back to São Paulo he became even more distant. He was clearly suffering from the trauma of the experience. It was so easy to understand. The place *was* a mess. What an awful thing for him to return to. Everything and everyone he loved there seemed to be in a sad state of deterioration.

"I had hoped to pick up the pieces when we got back to São Paulo, but by then communication with Flavio was impossible. He was cold, distant, and unapproachable. I was terribly concerned about him. The embarrassment brought on by his family's situation had really shaken him. It was a most unpleasant ending for me. When I went to say goodbye to him, he frowned and made a motion that meant 'get out of my way'. Then he turned and walked off. I was crushed. Suddenly he turned back toward me. I had hoped it would be for an instant of reconciliation.

" 'Send me my other marbles I left in Denver,' he said. That was the last I was to see of him."

Twelve

The atmosphere at the Protestant Mission was far more aus-
tere than that at Cheltenham, and Flavio's entrance there was
kept free of any publicity. Only the headmaster knew that
Flavio was the celebrated subject of two *Life* magazine stories,
and the headmaster wanted to keep it that way. So, for the first
time in two years, Flavio was just another student in a strict pa-
rochial institution.

Without the generosity and attention Flavio enjoyed at
Denver he became sharply aware of his failings and more tormented by the illusory hopes he had held for himself back in
America. He had proven that he could adjust to foreign situations—but it was easier to conform to good situations than to
bad ones. Flavio still thought of everything in Brazil as bad,
including the Mission school, and he rapidly regressed to the
old problems that had marred his first days at Denver. Once

more he became hostile to his classmates, refused to study, and was insolent to his teachers. The stern headmaster then denied him weekend recreational privileges until his behavior improved. José Gallo made three trips from Rio to São Paulo within six weeks to reason with Flavio and try to help him adjust.

To Flavio the worst punishment was to be confined to his room for the weekend while the other students went home, to the movies or on pleasure trips. One Saturday morning José found him sitting alone and disconsolate on his bed.

"I hate this place," Flavio complained. "Why didn't you get me into the American School in town? They wouldn't treat me like this."

"The American School refused to take you because they were afraid you would act just the way you are acting now," José told him bluntly.

This was a very special hurt to Flavio. He thought for a few seconds, then replied, "They must not be real Americans at that dumb school."

"You're making it hard for yourself by not living up to what you promised Reverend Bastos."

"They are idiots here. They don't understand me."

"They were kind enough to take you in. That's no way to talk about them."

"I want to leave this place. I'm sick of it already. Look. I'm the only kid left here. The rest of them are off having a good time someplace."

"That's because you were disobedient. Those instructors are here to teach you, and you are here to learn." José scanned the letter from the headmaster which had summoned him there. "It says here that your roommate moved out on you because of your awful attitude."

"Let him go. I didn't like him anyway. He was a tattletail."

Flavio spewed out his wrath to his third grade teacher the following Monday, saying angrily, "America is the only place to be. Brazilians are awful and this school is awful!"

The headmaster called Flavio in and warned him that if he didn't change his attitude toward the school, the students, and the teachers, he wouldn't be allowed back again. Less than a year after leaving America, where he had done so well, Flavio had again become intolerable. And it took nearly two months before the headmaster's inflexible attitude and José's gentle admonitions took hold and eventually eased Flavio into a sunnier disposition. Suddenly he began to study, but by then he had fallen far behind his class. He would never find the happiness he had known at Cheltenham, but his manner toward the other students softened to a polite aloofness; he worked and played mostly alone and, as always, avoided close relationships. Nevertheless, he became somewhat of a novelty after the not-so-well-kept secret about the *Life* stories leaked out. Furthermore, near the end of the school year, he did make one close friend, Evandro Luiz da Silva, a 26-year-old divinity student attending the school. From the beginning Evandro had tried to encourage Flavio and to give him friendly advice. He helped him with his assignments, corrected his Portuguese, and eventually arranged to have Flavio share his dormitory room. Evandro had one more year of study at the Mission School, after which he would transfer to a seminary to complete his studies for the ministry. He was engaged and was happily making plans for his forthcoming marriage, and this became the subject of many of their evening discussions.

Once Flavio spoke about having a wife of his own some day, and Evandro teased him, asking him what kind of wife he would want.

"She will have to be a good cook and beautiful and smart," Flavio answered.

"Then you will have to provide good food for her to cook, good clothes to compliment her beauty, and a good brain of your own to match hers."

"Oh, Flavio Luiz da Silva will do that. Don't worry."

Evandro laughed, picked up Flavio's final report card and waved it. "If you don't get better marks than these next year, no woman in her right mind will even look at you, let alone marry you."

"You will see. You will see. I already speak two languages, don't I? That is already something."

"It's how much you know in both languages that's important, not just that you speak them."

Flavio acknowledged Evandro's advice with a grin. He started pulling his clothes from a chest to pack his suitcase. José Gallo was coming the next morning to drive him back to Rio for the year-end vacation and Christmas holidays with his family. They were well down the highway when José broached the subject of Flavio's poor marks. Flavio cut him short. "I'd rather go to hell than go back to that school. It must be the worst school in all of Brazil!" he said angrily. José drove on without further comment.

The home Flavio returned to was still a shambles. There were twelve to sleep now instead of ten. The children were sleeping four to a bed again, some on the living room floor on makeshift pallets. Nair, swollen with yet another child, had taken to her bed with severe prenatal sickness. Pitching in, Flavio spent his first days there washing three years of grime from the walls, scrubbing and polishing the floors, washing the windows, repairing the furniture as best he could, getting the refrigerator working again, and persuading his brothers and sisters to accept regular household chores. Flavio once more did all the cooking, so that his mother could rest.

He had some welcome help from his friends in America. Phil

Vandevoort sent him fifty dollars and a collection of rare stamps. Irene Tatem also sent money and a notice that she had opened a savings account for Flavio with $65.00. He answered the letters promptly, telling about his "awful" first year at the Mission school and how much he hated it. He thanked them for the money and explained that he had spent some of it for an oil cloth for the kitchen table, two scrub brushes, a broom, laundry soap, three tubes of toothpaste, and a dozen tooth-brushes.

A week after Flavio's return José da Silva wrecked his truck. The father came home seething with anger, wondering how he would scrape up enough money for repairs. He had long before spent the money set aside by *Life* for his family's use. He scowled through most of the meal, and, spitting a mouthful on the floor, he shouted to Flavio, "That was a lousy dinner!"

"Then why don't you try cooking for yourself?" Flavio shouted back.

This earned Flavio a couple of hard thumps on the head and an order to "get out and find a job and bring in some money." José then stalked out of the house and slammed the door, not to return for a couple of days. Flavio turned the cooking over to Maria, the cleaning over to Mario and Luzia, and went job hunting. He got one delivering groceries, but the place went out of business after four days. He then became a machinist's helper at a local garage, but soon found out he wasn't strong enough to handle the heavy equipment. It was just as well because Nair had started to have labor pains. She went to the hospital early one Sunday evening. The baby came twenty-six hours later through a painful delivery. Shortly afterward, the doctor told her that her eleventh child was dead.

America's virtues were always on Flavio's mind and more than once his harping on the topic got him into trouble with the neighborhood boys during curbside discussions. As he described the wonders of New York one afternoon, Jaime Borges cut him off.

"Ah, da Silva, why don't you go back there if you like it so much," he said scornfully. "You are just trying to be taller than the rest of us because you went to the United States."

"You are a Americano king without money," Peitor Santos added.

Everyone laughed except Cleuza das Graças. Instead, she pointed her finger at Peitor and said, "You should listen to him. It's true when he says we Brazilians don't help each other. You just put each other down like you are doing now."

"What do you know about it, Cleuza?" Jaime Borges scoffed.

"I don't know much of anything, and neither do you, but at least I am willing to listen," Cleuza answered sharply.

Flavio was impressed with his pretty defender, with her courage, her big brown eyes, and long black hair. He had never seen her before, but from that day on he smiled warmly whenever he saw her. He carried her groceries and packages and took her on long walks. Soon Flavio da Silva was in love, and so was Cleuza das Gracas. The two of them had something in common. She too had been very poor and adopted into a family of fourteen brothers and sisters. When her stepfather died her mother married again; they had somehow escaped the favela, and all the children had gone to school. At fifteen, Cleuza already had the equivalent of a junior-high-school education. And this, perhaps more than anything else, gave Flavio second thoughts about wanting to go back to school and catch up. Evandro's warning about having a brain as good as his wife's was now well worth his consideration.

José da Silva's luck was still running low, and almost every day he and Flavio quarreled. One such confrontation took place in the presence of Cleuza one day when José bawled Flavio out for not cleaning some empty paint cans. The argument kept up until they reached the house, and José had pointed at it, shouting, "I'm going to sell this damned place and leave all of you!"

"You can go," Flavio shot back, "but you won't sell the house. There is a line in the document that keeps you from doing that."

"That is a lie! Come show me such a line."

And Flavio had stormed into the house and taken the deed from a drawer, found the line and started to read.

"I don't trust you," José said. "Let Batista read it."

When Batista read the clause José's anger peaked, and he threatened to beat everyone in sight. Most of the children hurriedly got out of his sight. Flavio stood his ground, saying, "I will be a man soon, and I will not stay with you any more."

"Okay! Get out anytime you like. The sooner the better!"

"I will. I promise you I will," Flavio screamed as José slammed the door in his face and marched out of the yard. More than ever now Flavio wanted to go back to school. He had made his choice between the two hells, and since there were only three weeks of vacation left he began packing his suitcase for his return to São Paulo.

Christmas slipped in so quietly that Flavio hardly knew when it arrived. Nobody in his family ever expected anything of it, or even discussed it. For Flavio, this year there would be no turkey, no snow, no beautiful tree with gifts beneath it. Only the memory of that magical day with the Gonçalves was left. On Christmas Eve Flavio decided to make a Christmas celebration for his brothers and sisters. He gathered several leafy limbs from a tree, tied them together and stuck them into a bucket of sand that served as a base. He bought some green and red wrapping paper and cut out tree decorations, sticking them to the makeshift tree with paste made from flour and water. From two grocery sacks he cut rectangles of paper and, with his crayons from America, made colorful cards for everyone in the family, and one of course for Cleuza. With the rest of the money Phil Vandevoort had sent, Flavio bought each one a small gift. He stuffed hard candy and peanuts into as many socks as he could find, and after everyone was asleep he put the socks and the presents beneath his tree.

The next morning he arose early and went from room to room shouting, "Get up! Get up! *Papaï Noel* has been here!"

On New Year's Cleuza promised Flavio that she would marry him—someday. And to him this was the best gift of all. But at the height of his happiness José Gallo came with a letter from the Reverend Moyses Bastos. José sat Flavio down with his parents and read the letter slowly:

Dear José,

At the request of Reverend Ruben Alberto, I am answering your letter of December 14. Reverend Alberto is on holiday, and asked me to wish you a happy and prosperous New Year.

We here at the mission realize just how much you have done to help the moral, spiritual, and intellectual formation of Flavio. But Flavio can no longer stay at our boarding school. We are sorry to have to give you this news, but there is no alternative. His behavior is not satisfactory and his schoolmates can no longer tolerate him.

Thanking you for your attention and preference for our school, I remain,

Sincerely,

Rev. M. Bastos
Vice-Director

José shook his head with disappointment. "Well, that is it," he said. Flavio was stunned. "What does it mean?" he asked, as though he hadn't understood a word José had read.

"It means that you have been kicked out of school, and that they won't take you back," José answered.

"But I want to go back," Flavio said. "Can't you do anything? I promise to do better this year."

"I'm sorry. It's too late. You had plenty of warning but you wouldn't listen. I've already appealed to the headmaster, but he will not give in."

"What about Evandro? Evandro can help."

"No one can help now, Flavio. You must understand it. It is too late."

Angry and disillusioned, Flavio walked out to the front porch. Nair turned to José Gallo. "What do we do now?" she asked.

"Flavio is a big boy now," he reminded her. "He must make up his own mind about his future. However, I think we should enroll him in a primary school and get him a private English teacher. I don't see any other way out." There was no other choice; Nair and her husband agreed.

But by now Flavio was far too old for his class level in public school, so two weeks later José enrolled him in a private school, the Abraham Lincoln School. The fact that the school was named after an American president pleased Flavio very much. "It is sure to be a better school," he assured Cleuza, "and I will be closer to you staying here." Cleuza accepted Flavio's setback more easily than he had expected. Buoyed by her attitude, Flavio promised to work even harder at his English and to teach it to her as well.

For the next two years Flavio did rather well at Abraham Lincoln. Besides history and geography, which he had come to like very much, he took courses in manual training and, as expected, he excelled in them. In the meantime, his love for Cleuza deepened; he kept the family going despite its inertia, and, still consumed by his love for America, he wrote to everyone back there who he thought might help him go back one day. Nair had another child; Maria and Luzia dropped out of school, and José sold his battered truck to a junk dealer. With yet another mouth to feed, and his pockets constantly empty, he became even more sullen and morose. Hardly a day passed without his getting into an argument with Flavio. The boy had gone to school long enough, he complained to Nair. He should get out now and help support the family with a steady job. Da Silva was not aware of the existence of Flavio's personal *Life* fund; he simply assumed the magazine was only paying for Flavio's schooling. José Gallo had been careful to keep Flavio's independent income a secret to prevent the father's making use of it, and he did his best to make the money last by doling it out to Flavio sparingly.

One evening, Flavio's father tried to keep him from going out to see Cleuza, and physical violence erupted. When Flavio persisted Da Silva hit him and shoved him against the wall. "If you go out that door you can't come back," he threatened.

"I'm a man now, and I pay my own way, so you don't tell me what to do. And if you hit me again, I'll tell the people at *Life* and they will get the police after you and kick you out of this house!"

Flavio's threat had its desired effect. Da Silva backed down. No doubt he reasoned that it was through Flavio and *Life* that he had got the house. Perhaps, if Flavio insisted, *Life* would throw him out. Da Silva settled with an impassioned order: "Get your stuff packed and get out of here tomorrow."

"I will. Believe me, I will," Flavio said as he marched out the door.

As they walked the streets that night Flavio and Cleuza decided they must do something about his unhappy life at home. Cleuza came up with what they both thought was a brilliant idea. Flavio should move into the extra room at her mother's house. There was plenty of space now since all Cleuza's brothers and sisters had married and moved out. They hurried toward her home, where Cleuza tried the idea out on her mother.

The next day, to José da Silva's astonishment, Flavio kept his word. He packed his belongings, kissed his mother goodbye, and moved one big step closer to his dream of making Cleuza his bride. At the end of his second year at the trade school he took his final examination and passed it. Within a month he had a job, again as a mechanic's helper. From then on he seldom went to his father's house, but when Batista came to tell him that Maria was leaving to work for a family in the northeast of Brazil, he went to say goodbye to her.

"How long will you stay?" he asked.

"I don't know," she answered. Then, smiling, she added, "Who knows, I might get married and never come back." That same morning Maria was taken away in a car. Neither parent knew her employer's name or where they were taking her. She was gone for a full week before Nair realized that Maria had not even left the address of her destination. All she could hope was that Maria would someday write and let them know her whereabouts.

Flavio was much happier now. He took on an extra job as a waiter's helper at a large restaurant. If he learned quickly enough, the owner told him, he could become a full-time waiter. He found it tough holding down two jobs, but his prestige rose rapidly at the restaurant when he began translating orders for English-speaking customers. The owner was impressed enough to give him a two-dollar-a-week raise. On his birthday in April, two months hence; Flavio would turn 21 and collect the remainder of the money in his *Life* fund.

On April 4, 1970, José placed $4,500.00, the balance left in the fund, in Flavio's personal bank account. That night Cleuza and Flavio set their wedding date for the following June. Cleuza's mother promised them the house as a wedding gift. She was going to live with one of her older sons who needed help with his children. Flavio's first move was to put a third of his money into repairs and alterations on the house. He painted both the exterior and the interior, enlarged the kitchen, and paved the backyard. He wanted everything ready for the wedding reception, hurrying home after his day's work at the machine shop to urge the workmen on, then going on to his other job at the restaurant.

Everything went off as Flavio planned. The alterations were completed in time. The wedding took place on the scheduled day and hour, at the Church of Our Savior. Both families and nearly fifty other guests attended. Flavio's little sister Rute was the flower girl and led the procession with Cleuza's nephew Juan. Cleuza wore white satin with a headpiece of lace, and carried fresh white flowers. It was a simple and lovely ceremony performed by a young priest from the Guadalupe Barrio district. Nair, looking rather perplexed, stood next to Cleuza's mother, whom she had met for the first time that day. José da Silva stood back in the dark of the church, alone, finding it hard to believe that this troublesome stepson would now be a married man and a property owner in his own right. At the end of the ceremony Flavio and Cleuza embraced and kissed; then, beaming with happiness, they fled to the church exit under a hail of rice. Flavio had most of what he wanted now—Cleuza and a home of their own. There was no more advice for José Gallo to give, no more records for him to keep or problems to solve. Flavio da Silva was on his own at last. He would now be the keeper of his own memoirs. And many years would pass, leaving only the memory of him to those of us who were once so close to him.

Thirteen

On the second day of August, 1976, I was in a Buenos Aires shop trying on a pair of shoes. One clerk, a large swarthy man with white hair, stared at me from the moment I entered the store. Something about me obviously bothered him; as he crossed the room that something snapped him about. He came toward me, an intent look on his face, saying, "I remember you now. You're the one who befriended the little boy in the favela many years ago."

"Yes, many years ago," I admitted.

"Is he all right? Is he still alive?"

"I'm sure he is all right," I said, realizing suddenly that I really wasn't so sure. Six years had passed since I had last heard any news of Flavio da Silva.

"What year did that happen?"

" 'Sixty-one." (Flavio; Rio; I began thinking. Both were only a short plane trip away, and José Gallo would surely know how to find him.)

"You took him to New York?"

"Denver, Denver, Colorado—to a clinic." (My business would be finished by nightfall. I could spend a week in Rio.)

"He must be a man now. Makes me feel old."

I decided to telephone José as soon as I got back to the hotel. It had indeed been a long time. Flavio's last letter had come to me ten years before, in October, 1967. The English was fair, the scribbled handwriting understandable but shaky:

> How are you my good friend Gordon Parks and how is your family? If I could see you I would be very happy. Do you remember the watch you gave me? It is broken and I don't know where I can get it fixed in Brazil. When you come to Brazil I want to talk to you about a lot of things. Dear Gordon could you help me get back to America? In São Paulo I lost the typewriter you gave me. Could you get me another one when you come back? I will always remember you and I hope you will always remember me. Your good friend, Flavio José Luiz da Silva.

I reached José Gallo late that same evening. He told me that he had not seen much of Flavio since 1970, but that he still lived in the Guadalupe district. He was still married and, José thought, had two children.

"I'll take the early morning plane."

"It will be good to see you. I'll be at the airport."

Fifteen years had passed since I had last seen Flavio, and as the plane touched down on the Rio landing strip the next morning, I thought it seemed even longer. José was there, smiling. We embraced warmly. His once-black hair was as thick as ever but now it was handsomely streaked with gray, and he had put on weight. He still had the weary look of those awful days we shared on the hillside of Catacumba.

We drove to my hotel that was located several miles south of the bustling Copacabana area. It overlooked a great sweep of beach and a blue-green sea that churned into the base of a rugged mountain. There were two swimming pools, two tennis courts, and acres of matchless green for golfing. But less than a mile southward, all this magnificence abruptly ended. There, the favela of Rocinha sprawled like a sore all over the side of the mountain, a favela so huge that, had Catabumba been placed inside it, it would have gone unnoticed. It seemed the favelas would always be with us.

Even before my bags were unpacked, José and I started off to find Flavio. As we drove along José reminisced about those first days we had spent in the favela, halting now and then to hurl insults at drivers speeding too close to his new Volks-wagen.

"*Filho da puta!*" he shouted, thrusting his thumb downward in a sign of obscene disgust. Then he turned to the subject of Flavio.

"I don't really know how we will find this boy," he said. "It has been some time since I have seen him. The last I heard he had a watchman's job, but he was also a waiter at a restaurant for a while."

The Guadalupe district, where we had bought the home for Flavio's family, seemed to be much farther away from Rio than I remembered. We drove for nearly an hour through heavy traffic, seeing other favelas along the way. Brazil's wealth was apparent in the teeming industrial areas we drove through; one newly built skyway that snaked into the heart of Rio looked to have cost at least a billion dollars. The clustered favelas seemed incongruous in the midst of such obvious prosperity.

José stopped for the final turn off the highway into the area where Flavio lived. A policeman who seemed half asleep stood at the intersection. He and José took lazy looks at one another, playing the familiar game of Brazilian bluff. José rubbed his chin, measuring the policeman's attitude.

"That dumb cop knows I want to turn left and he can't wait to tell me I can't do it, and for no reason at all. Just watch." The signal changed and José feigned a turning motion. The lethargic cop lifted his chin an inch and thumbed José straight ahead.

"Ah! *Filho da puta!* Such dumb cops!" José gunned his motor and we lurched forward and started circling the block for an approach from another intersection.

The block we eventually entered was uncommonly quiet. Two mangy dogs trotted in opposite directions down the rutted dirt street. A lone boy of about ten jerked at the string of a kite that had caught in the top of a coconut tree. An old woman tended a flower garden alongside her porch. The neat row of houses, painted in pastel pinks, greens, and blues, seemed to be slumbering under the warm August sun. They were all about the same shape—square bungalows surrounded with low concrete walls of the same pastel shades. There was a distinct feeling of cleanliness throughout the block. Not so much as a scrap of paper lay on the sidewalks or the street. Yet it was clear that the dwellers here had far more pride than they had money. Despite their vigorous color the houses had an air of struggle about them. Tall palm and coconut trees towering above the houses lent a tropical grace to this neighborhood, whose occupants obviously worked hard for a living. José fed more gas to the Volkswagen and we bumped over the curb, onto the sidewalk, and stopped. "This is it," José said dryly. "This is where he lives."

A tremor of guilt swept through me. There had been no way of notifying Flavio that we were coming; he had no telephone. I wouldn't have welcomed such a surprise. He had a right to resent our walking in on him unannounced. I took a hurried look at the house. It was painted a soft green. The tiny yard was as clean as a church pew. A locked wooden gate hinged to a concrete wall barred our way. José cupped his hands around his mouth. "Flav!" he shouted. A few seconds passed; then José called out again. The door opened and Flavio appeared. He looked hard at us, seeming puzzled, then startled for a moment. Then a smile broke over his face. He came toward us silently, and reached over the fence to embrace me.

"I cannot believe this. Gordon Parks, my friend," he said softly. "José, where did you find him?"

"He found me," José replied, smiling.

Flavio was now a handsome young man of twenty-seven. He was still small, about five-foot-six. His hair was neatly combed, and he wore a blue knit shirt and sharply pressed brown trousers. He was thin but there was a wiry toughness about him. Beneath the apparent frailty one sensed the tenacity of a fighting cock. The soft lines of his chilhood had hardened into manliness.

"Come in. Come in, Gordon Parks. My family has waited for so long to see you." We crossed the yard and entered the house. Inside, waiting, were Flavio's wife and two small children. He introduced them proudly. "This is my wife, Cleuza, and my sons, Flavio Junior, who is now four, and Felipe Luiz, who is one."

Cleuza stood smiling shyly. Her hair was still black and silky, and her eyes were a soft brown. Flavio Junior, unaware of the gravity of the moment, had become noisy and tugged at her skirt, pulling her toward the kitchen. Flavio reprimanded him gently but to no avail. Then Cleuza whispered a command. Junior fell instantly quiet. There had been a firmness in her voice that he obviously respected.

"So you are Flavio's lovely wife, Cleuza. I am glad to meet you," I said slowly.

Confused, she rubbed at her temples. "You lovely wife to meet, Cleuza?" she answered.

Flavio smiled and touched her cheek. "No, Cleuza, you are

my lovely wife and he is glad to meet you," he corrected her. He turned to me. "Her English is not so good yet."

"My wife you lovely wife!" She threw up her hands, laughing. "*Fala Portuguese,* Flavio! *Fala Portuguese!*"

"She gives up too easy. But she will learn. She is very smart. That is one reason I married her," Flavio said. A beautiful girl suddenly appeared in the kitchen doorway. "Gordon, do you remember this bad one?" he asked.

I searched the lovely, shy face, my mind racing backward over the years, over the dirty, hungry, and angry young faces of the Da Silva household. There was no resemblance to anyone I could remember.

"I give up. Who is she?"

Flavio spoke to her in Portuguese. "Say your name, silly girl. Tell Gordon your name."

The girl broke into an even shyer smile. "Isabel," she said in a near whisper.

Isabel! The scowling, clawing, ill-tempered Isabel, who had once sunk her teeth into me and stuck me with a rusty pin. Isabel, from whose little foot I had pulled the rusty nail that night in her father's shanty store after she had kicked me. The change was incredible. I gave her a hug. "You are the one I used to call the 'bitter flower'," I said. When Flavio translated my words she reddened and laughed. "Ask her if she remembers me, Flavio?"

"No, she will not. I have asked her many times before. She was only three then. She lives with me now, and she will some day amount to something, I am sure. That's why I have her with me."

Like the others, Isabel was clean and neatly dressed. The living room was small and sparsely furnished with a leatherette sofa and matching chair, a coffee table, a television set, and a new sewing machine. A large, hand-colored double portrait of Flavio and Cleuza hung on the pink wall. The coloring in it aged them another ten years. A reproduction of *The Last Supper* hung with several others on another wall. The place was immaculate and Flavio was obviously proud of it.

"Come," he said, "I will show you the rest of our house—our home. It is not much but you will see for yourself."

I remembered now how he had once said, "Some day I want to live in a real house, on a real street, with pots and pans and a bed with sheets." As we walked through this real house I realized he had achieved his dream. Each child had his own bed and closet. Flavio and Cleuza's bed was larger than the one his entire family had slept in back in the favela. All the bathroom fixtures, including a bidet, looked new. This was a far cry from the three wooden toilets at the bottom of Catacumba that served over 25,000 favelados. Flavio seemed proudest of the kitchen, with its array of shining pots and pans.

"This room used to be smaller, with just this much space," he said, pointing toward an alcove, "but I have made it much bigger, as you can see." He turned a knob on the stove and a blue flame rose. "Real gas and four places to cook. And how do you like the sink for washing dishes? It is good, yes?"

"Very good, Flav. Very good."

Next he took us to the backyard. "I had all this paved with concrete so that the boys don't get so dirty. I don't want Cleuza scrubbing clothes all the time." A large coconut tree shaded one corner of the backyard. He shinnied up the tree and hacked off two coconuts and threw them down to José. "We will drink some of the milk later if you like." There was also a small toolshed and a chicken coop. In it were several hens and a large, red rooster.

"The old cock and I fight all the time. Watch." He picked up a stick for protection and cautiously entered the coop. The rooster's feathers instantly ruffled as his head lowered into a fighting position. Flavio goaded him with the stick. "Come on, old cock, fight for my friends!" Flavio Junior and Filipe danced about gleefully. Watching their father fence with the rooster was obviously one of their daily entertainments. The rooster made a couple of halfhearted lunges, then retreated to a neutral corner. "He's lazy today. Had too much corn. No fight in him," Flavio said. To the children's disappointment, he came out of the coop.

As we walked back into the kitchen José shook his head and smiled. "It is amazing that his English is so good after so many years. His Portuguese is also much better," he said.

For the next hour Flavio talked about the friends he had left in America and the school and Institute at Denver. He pulled out boxes of letters that had come to him from the States. There were dog-eared postcards and letters from people he had never seen, several from Phil Vandevoort and one from Tommy Ebbe. "Boy, was that Tommy a crazy one. I wonder where he is now."

"Living in California, I hear. He also has a son," I said.

Flavio bent over with laughter. "Crazy Tommy Ebbe with a son? I can't believe it." The largest package of letters was carefully wrapped in cellophane. He pulled them out and handed them to me. Fifty or more of them dated back through the early 1970's to 1961. They were all posted from Schenectady, New York.

"They are from Miss Irene Tatem," he said. "Did you know her?" I didn't, but I had heard the name before. "She is dead now," Flavio added. Suddenly I remembered. Her estate had sent me photographs of herself and Flavio in a small silver frame shortly after her death. "You are to keep these forever," was the instruction in the will.

"She was a very good friend," Flavio continued, "and somewhere in a bank where she lived there is money for me. Read this. It says so right here." The letter, postmarked in March, 1970, confirmed that she had deposited another $50.00 in his savings account. "Do you think you can help me find the bank somehow? There should be some interest on my money by now?" I promised to make inquiries when I got back to New York.

"You look very tired," José said.

"I sleep in the day and work in the night as a guard. That is why. It is a tough job but better than being a waiter," Flavio said.

Flavio talked about his job. Ironically, he who had known poverty at its worst was now employed to watch over the life of a rich man's son. Flavio perhaps preferred it to that of being a waiter because it lent him the kind of authority that went with the huge revolver he carried on his bony hip. His client, a wealthy Brazilian with a grand house on several acres of wooded land outside Rio, feared that his child might be kidnapped. Flavio, with his gun, was hired to prevent that. His patrol lasted from seven each night until seven the next morning. When the winter sun dropped beneath the mountains, the chill fog swept in and Flavio tramped the outer perimeter of the estate all night, pumping his arms to keep warm, munching cold sandwiches and smoking packs of cigarettes to kill the boredom. When the relief guard arrived, Flavio turned over his weapon and walked a mile to the bus that would take him home. For this he got 1,700 cruzeiros a month ($160).

José and I had left shortly after, despite Flavio's protests. He was wound up in recalling the best days of his life. I assured him that we would come again, that we would have plenty of time to talk before I left for New York. We could see that he needed rest badly. "You can also come by my hotel after work any morning you like. We will have breakfast and talk as much as you want," I promised. Flavio and Cleuza followed us out to the gate. As I got into the car I mentioned that I would like to visit his parents and his other brothers and sisters. Flavio's face clouded, and shaking his head, he said, "I'm afraid my father is the same. Always the same. My mother and the others—well, things are not so good." He forced a smile. "We will talk about that at breakfast."

A sadness had swept over him at the mention of his family. Some of the joy that had come with our reunion slipped away.

The traffic was even heavier on the way back to the city. Both José and I were silent until he inched his way into the stream of speeding cars. "Well, what did you make of it?" José finally asked.

"I was impressed and very happy until the end when he began talking about his parents. I think Flavio is trying hard. He's no roaring success but so much better off—a nice wife, two healthy children, a house of his own, and a job."

José took time to digest my words before answering. "Yes, but things could be so much better for him. I tried to tell that boy how to manage things better, but he wouldn't listen. For instance, I tried to get him to keep his waiter's job. In that way he could meet more interesting people eat better food, and perhaps get a promotion." José yawned and rubbed his chin; I waited for him to go on. "I even told him he could save his money and buy a taxi, or start a little cafe of his own. Not a big one, mind you, just a little hole in the wall that could grow into something larger. I don't think he even listened to me. I was worried about giving him the money left over from his fund after he became twenty-one. I was afraid he was going to throw it away."

"How long did it actually last?" I asked.

"Three months at the most. Then it was all gone. But then he was a man, and we had no control over how he spent it." José shook his head. "I think he shot himself in the leg with that gun he carries around at night."

"Really? Are you sure of that?"

"Pretty sure. He would never admit it, but one of the people at the security company hinted as much."

"But he doesn't limp."

"He was lucky as hell he didn't do more damage. He was just laid up for several weeks."

As we neared the city, traffic became increasingly heavy. The constant beeping of horns in front and in back of us set up an awful din. Conversation became impossible. I sat back and thought about how we had found Flavio, quietly happy and in good health. The cleanliness of him, his family, and his home reflected the earlier training at Willens. Yet there had been an uneasiness in his manner, moments when he seemed on the verge of saying something, but frowned slightly and spoke of something else. We would be alone, I thought, and I would ask him about those leftover things in his past, not necessarily secret things, but those things that were unresolved and worth talking about. Perhaps then he would tell me what was bothering him.

The telephone jarred me awake at 7:30 the next morning. I covered my head with a pillow, hoping it was a wrong number. But the caller was insistent; the phone kept ringing. Irritated, I fumbled through the half-darkness for the receiver. "Who is it?" I asked brusquely.

"Mr. Gordon Parks, this is your good friend, Flavio da Silva."

"So early? Where in hell are you?"

"Downstairs in your hotel. I have come to have breakfast and talk about America."

"My good friend Flavio da Silva, I am going to put my foot up your bony ass for waking me so early."

"No, no, you don't do that to good friends," he answered, laughing.

"Okay. Go to the restaurant and get something to eat. I will shower and come down to join you."

"No, no, I will not eat without you. I will wait."

"Okay. I'll be down without a shower. Order me a fresh

orange juice and a couple of toothpicks to prop my eyes open."

The pattern was set. I knew that I could expect that 7:30 call each morning for the week I would be in Rio. And despite my grumbling, I was quite pleased about it. We had orange juice, ham and eggs, and fresh fruit. The fruit was piled high on a separate table, and one selected a plate and served himself. I was about to place a banana alongside some sliced oranges and strawberries when Flavio objected.

"Don't put unpeeled bananas on the plate with the other fruit. The skin is always dirty," he warned. Impressed, I looked about the restaurant, scanning the plates of the other breakfasters. As I suspected, Flavio and I were the only ones with quarantined bananas.

"Flavio," I said, "there are a lot of people in here dirtying up their fruit with those bananas."

"They are pigs," he said, smiling. "They do not know what is good for their health."

Flavio looked fresher this morning, even though he had just come from work. His hair was neatly groomed and his complexion was still ruddy from the night air. He smiled as we began to eat. "I just can't believe you are back again," he said. "I have told my family so much about you. Now they know you are a real-live person and not a dream I talked about."

I complimented him on his progress and his family, and this pleased him. Cleuza was indeed a good wife who had lived up to all his expectations. He talked of giving her and his sons a much better life and of their accomplishing things he as a child never even thought of doing; things such as going to a university to study medicine or perhaps law.

"Now you see the importance of education, Flavio."

"Oh, I have for a long time. I just made mistakes."

"At São Paulo, for instance," I said rather pointedly.

He frowned and attempted to wave the subject away with his fork. "Let's not talk about that place, Gordon. It was cold

there. The people were so different from those in America. I
hated everything there. I don't know why. I think José made a
mistake by sending me there. He should have got me a good
job instead."

"But the whole purpose was to educate you so that some day
you could get a better job. José was right; furthermore, he had
no choice."

"I suppose so. Anyway it was a lot better than staying at my
father's house. The first night I came back there from America
it was terrible. Oh, the goddamned noise! I couldn't stand the
noise and the dirt. It was awful to have to sleep in the corner
on the floor after having my own bed and clean sheets. After
one night there I was glad to go anyplace. When we left for
São Paulo the next day I was so glad to go."

"What went wrong at the school?"

"Nothing. They just didn't understand me. The boys were
jealous because I had been to America. I hate thinking about
it now. Why should they be so jealous of me for going to
America?"

I didn't have the answer; so I shifted the conversation to
what I knew he was eager to talk about. I asked him what he
liked so much about his two-year stay in the United States.

His eyes lit up, sparkled. "Everything!" he said. "The people were so good to me. And I liked learning the new language. Do you know I learned English so quick that everybody was very surprised. I remember Mrs. Hansen with her
crazy apples and onions—'Say onion. Say apple. Finger, say
finger.' It was crazy but it was lots of fun." Almost in a dream
he talked of all the other things—the presents, the ballgames,
the parades, picnics, and outings with the Gonçalves boys,
until at last we found ourselves alone in the restaurant.

The telephone rang as we entered my room. I picked up
the receiver. "José," I said. Flavio quickly pressed his finger
to his lips and shook his head. He didn't want José to know he

was there. This puzzled me, but I obeyed his wish. Later I asked him why he didn't want José to know.

"I just want to say things to you that he might not understand."

"José has been very good to you."

"Very good, much better than my father. But this morning I want to say things to you in my own way. Understand?"

"I do," I assured him.

He looked down to the pool area from my window. "It's beautiful down there. Can we go sit in the chairs by the water like the others are doing?"

"Of course," I said.

We left my room then, talking all the way down. And as we walked, I thought back to our stroll together down the Rio streets in search of the boys' store where we had bought his first pair of shoes. That had been seventeen years before. It was difficult to realize that this was the same boy grown into a mature man, walking again beside me.

At the pool area we settled into lounge chairs. Flavio took in the bathers and surroundings casually. "These people must be very rich," he said. Then abruptly he was back in America. "I was happy to be going on that plane with you that first night, but I was scared, too. I kept saying to myself, 'where are these people taking me to?' I just couldn't imagine where I was going way up there in the sky. It was like a strange story. At the hospital that first day I was really frightened, all those doctors saying things I couldn't understand." He laughed. "I thought they were going to chop me up and feed me to the pigs. They all looked like policemen in white uniforms."

"Do you remember not taking your clothes off until I took off mine?"

"Oh, yes, I remember. I thought somebody might steal my pants and shoes. I figured that if they stole yours too then we would both be standing there naked. I wasn't so dumb, huh? Oh, I was so happy with those shoes. When they cut them up I thought it was the most terrible thing in the world." He paused, scratched his head, and smiled. "You know I lost those pants at Denver and I never did find them."

"Why were you so afraid?"

"Everything was so strange and different, the language and everything. I didn't know if I would ever see my brothers and sisters again. I didn't know where anything was in that great big place, and people were leading me around from one place to another, putting me in rooms with strange machines and all kinds of colored lights. It was scary. Then they would bring in this doctor from Argentina. They thought we could talk together. But I couldn't understand him and he couldn't understand me. He probably thought I was an idiot and I thought he spoke very awful Portuguese. It was crazy . . . just crazy."

"Didn't you realize the doctors were trying to save your life?"

"I thought they were trying to kill me!" he said, laughing aloud. "They were sticking needles into me and poking their fingers in my mouth and ears. 'Bend over,' they would say, and poke my behind. 'Say ah! Jump up and down! Hold your breath! Lay down! Stand up!' They hit my knees and made them jump. They even tickled the bottom of my feet with a rubber hammer. 'These crazy policemen are nuts,' I kept thinking to myself. One day one of them stuck a stick down my throat and got my breakfast all over his uniform. Boy was he mad! The next time he put that stick down my throat he stood a long way from me, and I didn't blame him." The memories were flooding in now, relaxing him into a nostalgic mood. "It was a long time before I began to feel like everything was going to be okay. Then I knew everybody was trying to help me get well. When José Gallo sent me the pictures of my family and the new baby, I felt real happy—for a little while."

I hailed a waiter and ordered two Cokes. When they arrived Flavio offered to pay for them. I objected, but he insisted. It was a treat from him to me. The price took him aback. "These people who stay here *must* be rich," he said, scratching his head. "I feed my family for almost a week for what these Cokes cost."

"Next time you won't be so anxious to pay," I said.

"Oh yes I will," he answered. "I know your room number now. I'll just sign and charge it to 1516." He was catching on fast.

Flavio was quiet for a while, gazing out to sea. Then, as if he had been dreaming, he returned to reality, spoke in Portuguese, caught himself and switched to English. "I want you to know something very important." His brow puckered into seriousness. "When I got kicked out of the São Paulo school and came back home, it was like starting all over again. It was almost as bad as the favela. But I still wanted to learn. I liked history and geography and the Bible. I was really doing my best, Gordon. I hope you believe me. But my mother was always sick and I did all the cooking and washing and looking out for the small kids. They never got enough to eat at home then. My father was always picking fights with me and fussing about my getting a job. But I didn't know anything. I got a laborer's job, but it was too big for me. I just couldn't carry those big heavy pipes and machinery they wanted me to carry. So I got fired. But I wanted to make something out of myself so I wouldn't disappoint you and everybody who helped me. I wanted to invent things and work on airplanes or study animals and insects." There was a long pause. He was obviously about to say what he had come to say. The concerned look of the day before had returned to his face.

He phrased the first part of it as a question: "Do you believe what I have told you?" he asked simply.

"Yes I do, Flav," I answered.

The rest came out very quickly and directly. "Then, Gordon, I would like to go back to America. Please help me do this. In America I can live better and do something with my life and my family's life. I feel like an animal in a trap here."

I hardly dared to consider this futile wish of his, knowing that without the notoriety and financial help he had once enjoyed, without the strongest sense of responsibility, it would be impossible for him to survive back in the United States.

As if reading my mind, Flavio now spoke pleadingly. "I have friends in America who want me. I can stay with them while I study and learn. Then when I have a good job I can send for Cleuza and the children. That is how it would work, Gordon."

I knew of the friends he referred to. But he seemed to have forgotten that Irene Tatem, his elderly benefactor from Schenectady, was dead, and that Phil Vandevoort was not financially able to assume such a responsibility. Most of the staff who had befriended him at the Institute had long since left the place. These people were now scattered all over the world. His little friends, Tom Ebbe, Jimmy Gaddy, Mitsu, and the others were no doubt struggling to care for their own now. José Gonçalves's family still lived in Denver but he hadn't heard from them for a long time. Kathy, for some reason she herself couldn't figure out, had stopped writing. Dr. Falliers was now in private practice. When I revisited the clinic in 1976 only one doctor remained who recalled ever having seen Flavio, and he had never attended him.

I carefully expalined all this to Flavio, saying finally that even *Life* magazine had gone. But what was so clear to me made no sense to Flavio. As far as he was concerned, his friends were still there, "someplace in America," and they would never forget him. It seemed impossible for him to grasp that there were those who would always care *about* him, without being able to responsibly care *for* him.

"If only my father had let me stay there I would be somebody by now. Don't you believe so? I just know that all the people who helped me once will help me again. I am sure. If I could only get back there you would see."

His yearning was honest, poignant. He would go on believing that only in America could he have another chance. He got up to leave, drained, yet hopeful that he had got his message across, that perhaps I would in some way help. We walked slowly through the hotel lobby and out to the bus stop. As the vehicle approached us from the distance, he turned and made a confession, one that must have been difficult for him. "I never told anyone this before," he said, "but I almost did something terrible just to keep from coming back to Brazil."

"What was that, Flav?"

"I had a chance to steal Mrs. Hansen's car and run off. The car was right outside the school door and the key was in the dashboard with the motor running. I was thinking, 'I don't want to go back—no, I don't want to go back.' I thought about it for a minute or two and then changed my mind."

"Why?"

"It would have made too many problems for Mrs. Hansen and for you an all the people who helped me—even the police. I hated it but I knew that there was nothing I could do but come back."

The bus was upon us now. It screeched to a halt. Its doors opened like jaws and swallowed him up. As it roared off down the highway, I could still see Flavio moving toward the back, waving to me as he went.

Flavio and Cleuza take their wedding vows, June, 1970.
(*photographer unknown*)

Nair da Silva, 1977. (*Gordon Parks*)

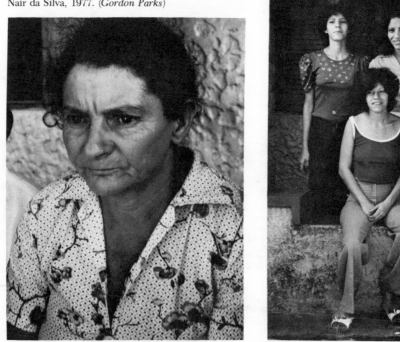

Flavio and Flavio Junior, Cleuza, Isabel and Felipe Luiz.
Guadalupe District, 1977. (*Gordon Parks*)

Flavio, his mother and brothers and sisters, 1977.
(*Gordon Parks*)

Isabel, 1961, age three. (*Gordon Parks*)

Isabel, 1977. (*Gordon Parks*)

Albia and Isabel, the favela, 1961.
(*Gordon Parks*)

Albia and Isabel, 1977.
(*Gordon Parks*)

Luzia, the favela, 1961. (*Gordon Parks*)

Luzia and her daughter, 1977. (*Gordon Parks*)

Flavio in his chicken coop. (*Gordon Parks*)

Flavio and Jose Gallo, 1977. (*Gordon Parks*)

Flavio Junior in tree and Felipe Luiz, 1977. (*Gordon Parks*)

Flavio, 1977. (*Gordon Parks*)

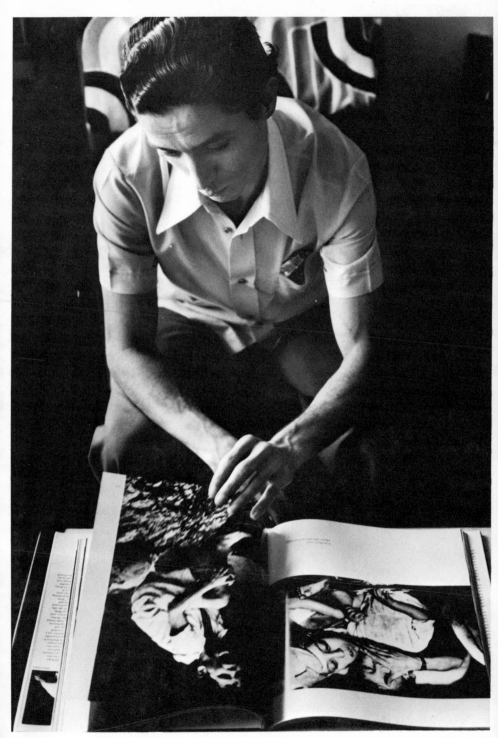

Flavio. (*Gordon Parks*)

Two days later Flavio took José and me to his father's house. The setbacks in that family's fortunes were apparent as we walked through the gate. The front yard that had once held flowers and other greenery was now as dull and scarred as a deserted battlefield. With José Gallo, who had driven us, we entered with a feeling of anxiety. Several children, none of whom I recognized, sat around the living room in a disorderly rubble of broken furniture. Flavio asked one child to find their mother. At the same time, Nair, looking twenty years beyond her age, came from the kitchen. She looked to be pregnant once again. Only her nose remained handsome on her now ruined face. She recognized me instantly and we shook hands. Soon all the other children had drifted in. Their father was noticeably absent. All of them viewed me with microscopic interest, as if they were awaiting some unusual gesture from this Americano who had once befriended their eldest brother. I stared back at them, trying hard to recall a memory of their faces sixteen years ago. *"Bom dia,"* I finally brought myself to say. Several of the older ones returned my greeting. The smaller ones continued to stare at me with greedy curiosity.

Now surprises came as Flavio identified them for me, from the oldest downward. "Here's Mario, the bad one who used to give me all the trouble. He is much the same." Mario stared, blankly, remembering nothing of me. "And this is Luzia. You must remember her getting slapped in the face with a fish by Maria. Those are her children standing next to her." Luzia smiled. She had lost some of her prettiness. Suddenly she remembered the perfumed oil I had given to Maria. When Flavio translated for her, she blushed darkly.

"Does she remember being angry and spitting at me for that?"

Flavio repeated my question to her. She rubbed her brow,

trying to recall the incident. "No, I can tell she doesn't," he volunteered. "Remember Batista?"

"Of course. Does he remember me?" He didn't. Nor did he recall that terrible moment when he had been so close to death beneath the car wheels. He was still darker than the others, and less handsome now. "He's still my father's favorite," Flavio said, shrugging his shoulders. Isabel suddenly arrived and she and Albia sat together, smiling shyly. They had been ages four and three when I had last seen them together, covered with flies and filth. They sat now, each much prettier and cleaner, far removed from the troubled portrait my mind had held of them for so many years.

"And, believe it or not, this is Zacarias, that baby I used to bathe in the dishpan. Look at him now. He couldn't even get his big foot into it." Zacarias, now seventeen, stood limply in the doorway, a detached glimmer in his eyes. Flavio singled out the smaller ones. "These have all come since you were here last—Celia, Rute, Daniel, Debora and Tereza." José had kept Nair busy. "Maria is up Northeast someplace, maybe with the family she went to work for. Maybe she's married. We haven't heard from her for over six years." Flavio threw up both hands. "Well, that's it. That's all of them," he said.

Nair moved painfully across the room and back to her kitchen. I followed her and motioned to José. Varicose veins coursed her legs, the legacy of the fifteen children she had borne. Whatever her failings, she had given all she had to give.

"Everyone is here but Maria," I said to her.

"I pray for her. She must have forgotten us." Nair, who talked very little, spoke with sadness. Flavio explained their circumstances. All the other children were staying at the house except Isabel. José da Silva was seldom home any more. When he came it was to take away part of the 600 cruzeiros ($60.00) Nair earned each month washing clothes.

Flavio shrugged, "I give what little I can every now and then. Five of them sleep in one bed, and five others in that bed next to them. Two sleep in the living room, one on the sofa, the other on the floor. When Maria and my father were here, fifteen of us were sleeping in this little place."

The truth came hard as I walked through the house. Most of the original furniture they had inherited with the house had either disappeared or been battered beyond repair. It puzzled me that some of the worst of it appeared to be plastered over by strips of wrapping paper that had been stuck on, obviously to hide dirt and scratches. The stove and frigidaire that Nair had been so proud of looked as if they had come from a junk yard. All the walls were badly smudged. The backyard paving was now cracked and sunken into the earth. Fifteen years of failure showed there beneath a dripping wash. The throwback to a state close to their former one was hard to accept. Flavio was plainly embarrassed, and it was understandable. All the hopes he had entertained for his family years before were now bankrupt.

I said good-bye, and we left that place as quickly as possible. I felt as if I were escaping a disaster, wondering meanwhile what all the once friendly neighbors thought of this blight on their otherwise spotless neighborhood.

As though he were trying to offset the disillusion of our visit to his father's place, Flavio invited José and me to his house for a *feijoada*, Brazil's most celebrated dish. I hung around the kitchen watching Cleuza, Isabel, and Flavio chop pork, beef, and onions while he explained how to cook the rice properly, boil black beans to the required tenderness, and mix spices into the rich bean sauce. He got out a white tablecloth, set the table expertly, and folded paper napkins beside each plate. Then we all proceeded to enjoy one of the very best *feijoadas* I have ever eaten. In response to the compliment he pointed to Cleuza. "Give her the credit. It is she who taught me to be a good cook—and a good husband." Cleuza must have understood, for she blushed and smiled her thanks.

As we ate Flavio reminisced, starting with a poignant and nostalgic glimpse of that first Christmas he spent with the Gonçalves family. "That beautiful tree with red and green lights. It was so beautiful. I got up early with Mark, Rick and Neil that morning, and we slipped in to see everything before their mother and father got up. It was like a big dream, all the presents I got from everywhere. And what a big dinner we had—turkey, ice cream and cake, pie, nuts—everything! Christmas is the best holiday in the world."

"Do your boys enjoy it?" José asked.

"Oh yes, I tell them there is a *Papai Noel*. It is good for them to believe for the first ten years because there is so much happiness for them to expect, and they will work harder if they think *Papai* will bring them something special."

Flavio paused, reflected, and changed the subject to his memories of Willens House. "You know I tried to like everybody and do what everyone wanted me to do. But it would make me mad when some smart guy laughed at me because I didn't know how to eat with a knife and fork. I wanted to crack the smart guy on his head. You understand? It was hard to tell who liked me at first because I didn't know English. I only guessed by their looks and the sound of their voices. Sometimes their voices didn't sound so good. It was hard for me at first, very hard. If I was angry about something, nobody understood me. So sometimes I made a big fuss to make them understand me. Sometimes it worked, sometimes it didn't work."

Later, over a dessert of fresh coconut, Flavio spoke about being away from his family during those early days in America. "At first it was just terrible. I almost forgot they

were living because I never heard from them. It hurt me bad
when my brothers and sisters didn't let me know they got the
gifts I sent them. I got to the point where I never wanted to
come back home. I didn't feel any love back here for me. I
think I was all mixed up like those beans we just ate," he said,
laughing. Turning serious again, he said, "I am very sorry for
what you saw at my father's house."

Flavio led us out to his backyard again. The contrast between his father's place and his was clearly discernible. He
didn't speak of the difference. He knew, as well as we, that it
wasn't necessary. Flavio was trying. Obviously, he wasn't as
happy as he had been in Denver. He seemed somewhat lost,
a little frustrated, but he was not bitter. Obviously, he was
striving for a better life for his wife and children.

"Perhaps it wasn't so terrible after all," I thought. For all
the forlorn decay of their house, even his brothers and sisters
were still healthier and far better off than they would have
been in the favela. More important, there was a school only a
few hundred feet away, something they would never have had
in Catacumba. So far, all of them had taken advantage of it. As
Nair wished, all of her older children would now read and
write.

A heavy gray fog blanketed the city the next morning when
Flavio, José and I set out for the favela of Catacumba. As we
drove along, I sensed an unusual quiet in both of them. I
glanced at Flavio, suddenly worrying about reawakening his
awful past. Yet he had been eager to come along, arriving an
hour before our departure.

A mist hung over the lagoon as we approached it, giving it a
pearl-gray luster that matched the day. I remembered well
the lovely sweep of water that divided the shacks of the favelados from the radiant white homes of the rich. We slowed

and José pulled to the side of the road and stopped. This was where I had first spotted the Christ figure towering over the mountainside of Catacumba seventeen years before.

I got out and looked skyward. Christo Redentor was still there, strongly silhouetted against the darkening clouds. Now I looked just below it. The favela of Catacumba was no more. Where once there had been thousands of shanties clinging to the mountainside, there were now only acres of unkempt tropical foliage. It was staggering. I stood for a moment looking in disbelief.

"It is all gone, Gordon," Flavio said, getting out of the car.

"It is so strange, so strange," I said. Both José and Flavio smiled at the shock on my face.

We piled back into the car, and skirting the far end of the lagoon, came at last to where the entrance of the favela used to be. Now there were rows of billboards advertising the glories of several airlines. Flavio got out and immediately made his way across the street. José and I followed. Pointing upward, he said, "That's where our house used to be." It was hard to imagine now that anyone, other than mountain goats, could have inhabited that treacherous looking slope.

"Come on. Let's climb," Flavio said.

We crawled under the billboards and started up, struggling through the tangled undergrowth. Several yards in, we heard muffled voices to our left. Two withered black women and a white, one-legged squatter stood in front of their shanty, which was half-buried in the foliage. They stopped talking and eyed us suspiciously as we passed.

Soon it was tough climbing. It looked as though the departed favelados had even taken the concrete steps they had built. The steep roadways that had once snaked upward between the shanties were now covered with slippery weeds. Now and then we came upon rocks that had been beaten into the earth for steps. The open ditches that served as sewerage channels were still soggy, but the mud was clean; green foliage blanketed the rot, and the stench was gone. It was as if everything—the shanties, sewer pipe, paths, and power lines they had worked so hard to construct—had mysteriously vanished into the earth.

We continued climbing, and the harder it became the faster Flavio seemed to go. He moved with the ease of an animal used to the feel of such a slope, climbing as though some magnetic force pulled him. Before long he had outdistanced José and me by a hundred feet.

"Come on you guys," he kept shouting. When, after nearly an hour, we reached the top, he was standing and gazing up at the Christ figure, seemingly caught in reverie. "This is it," he said, simply, when we reached his side. "This is the spot where we used to live."

The three of us sat there for a long time, tired, wordless, remembering what this spot meant to each of us. With all the voices gone, the quiet was incredible. The silence of those who had died on Catacumba mingled with the silence of those who had escaped it. Only a soft wind murmured through the tall weeds. Where were all the old and their young with the hungry faces, the cripples, the mangy dogs and skeletal cats? And why had we come back to this tomb of bad memories, other than to recall its misery?

I finally broke the quiet. "Where did they all go, and when?" I asked José.

"Most of them were moved to settlement houses built back in October, 1970. They're scattered all over—in Penha, Cordovil, and Jacarepagua. About a thousand families stayed in nearby Quitungo-Guaporé." José pursed his lips and shrugged. "So that was the last of it. Lacerda finally kept his word."

"How do you feel now about the eight years of work you and others put in here?"

"Catacumba's gone. But there's still a lot of others like it around. I think all the publicity about this one put it on the priority list. But it's gone, and I'm glad it's gone." As we got up and started back down, he added, "But I have faith that our self-help program will be carried on by the favelados from here, wherever they go."

The descent was no less difficult than the climb had been. Halfway down we spotted two traps set for wild animals. They were crude wooden boxes with trap doors, baited with rotted bananas and oranges. Obviously they had been set by the squatters down below. Flavio knew the kind of game they were after. "*Gamba* ("skunk") and armadillo is what they hope to catch," he said. "They are very good eating if you are lucky enough to catch one."

It had taken two-and-a-half hours for the climb to the top and the descent. As we drove away I turned for one final look, still amazed at how nature had so thoroughly reclaimed that poisonous mountainside. All that was left of it now were the tall weeds, two withered black women, a one-legged white squatter, and a couple of animal traps.

The final day of my visit was a gloomy one. It had rained continuously for twelve hours. At noon Flavio and I sat in my room eating hamburgers and observing the hunchback mountain outside my window. Looming high above the beach, it seemed to be crumbling under the heavy downpour. The sea crashed in against the towering cliffs.

"It's a bad day for you to leave," Flavio said, lighting his tenth cigarette.

"You smoke too much, Flav."

"I know. I will stop soon." He picked up the tattered *Life* magazine that I had brought with me, the issue that contained his story, and started thumbing through it. He came to the picture of himself stuffing food into baby Zacarias's mouth and

studied it for several moments. His brow wrinkled as he
turned slowly from page to page, coming at last to a picture of
himself lying ill on the sheetless bed. The caption beneath it
read: "Wasted by bronchial asthma and malnutrition, Flavio
fights a losing battle against death."

He closed the magazine and looked blankly out toward
the mountain again, a pensiveness settling over his face. "I
was sure going to die if you had not come."

"Possibly not."

"Oh yes, I knew. I didn't know what death was, but I knew
something bad was happening to me. I was so sick sometimes,
I guess I didn't care. I just worried about how my brothers
and sisters would live without me—with me dead." He
opened the pages again to a scene of their shack perched on
the mountainside. He looked at it for a long moment. "It's a
shame. My father's house is like the favela again. You saw for
yourself the other day. All those kids living with my poor
mother, who still cooks and slaves for them like she used to.
And they don't lift a finger to help her. Luzia's two children
never had real fathers. Only she knows who they are." He
stood up and walked to the window, smacked his hands
together. "I go over there sometimes and I get so mad I want
to spank all of them. My mother protects them. Well, I don't
want to have a fight with my mother because she had trouble
enough. If you think the place was bad when you saw it; then
you should have seen it the day before. I had almost to fight
with them to hide the filth and clean things up."

Now I understood the strips of paper that covered some of
the furniture. Flavio had pasted it there to conceal the dirt.
"My father is no help—he never has been. He lives far away
and only comes to take my mother's wash money. I try to get
her to hide it from him, but she won't. Some nights I can't
sleep for worrying about all of them. I guess that's why I
smoke so much. But I have my own family now and I must

surely look after them. You see for yourself that I do. I will keep trying to help my mother too. But one single *andorinha* ('swallow') can't make a summer."

Flavio was quiet now, and flushed with anger. He had said in a few words all that I had for so long wondered about. He stood up, spent by his own heated frankness. "I must go now," he said. "I must sleep some so I can be at the airport with you tonight."

We walked down the hallway without speaking. Everything I was tempted to say felt wrong. And he, at least for the moment, was talked out. The elevator, which usually took forever, shortened my discomfort by arriving immediately.

"Wait. I almost forgot something," he said. Holding the elevator door open with one hand, he reached into a shopping bag, pulled out a small package, and gave it to me. "This is from Cleuza and me. Open it on the plane. Okay?"

"Thanks."

"Tonight. I will see you tonight, Gordon."

"Tonight, Flav."

When José and I reached the airport, Flavio, Cleuza, and Isabel were already there. I was happy that they had come. But how to say goodbye? When the flight was announced, I decided I would simply say, "So long, Flavio. I must be going," and walk away as quickly as possible.

It didn't happen like that. Our last conversation became more awkward than the waiting.

"Isabel, you be a good girl now."

"*Si.*"

"I will never forget that wonderful feijoada, Cleuza. Tell Felipe and Flavio Junior goodbye for me."

"*Si.*"

"I will miss you, Flavio, my good friend."

"And I will miss you. You won't forget to write, will you?"

"I won't. And you be sure to answer."

My flight was called. "Well, that's it, Flavio," I said.

Flavio pulled me aside, away from the others. "I think almost every day about going to America, Gordon," he said softly, "to see the places that I once passed and to find all the friends that I know. It would be so good to have a job and live there again. Please, Gordon, see if you can get me back there."

The longing in his eyes was unbearable. I wanted to say finally, "Flavio, stop dreaming of going back. Those places you passed are too far away; those friends you knew are too scattered." I actually said, "I will try, Flavio. I promise I will try," and I hurried on, waving, leaving him once again, not even daring to hope for another miracle.

As the plane became airborne a depression swept over me. I had evaded Flavio's plea in a cowardly manner. Yet, I couldn't respond to his desire to return to a place that existed only in his memory. I felt that I had already shuffled his dreams too much. Those of us who had in some way touched his life witnessed an incredible experience. But now I was asking myself what that experience really meant. The miracles of energy that took place on Catacumba were dissipated; it was as though they had never been. The Da Silva family was better off, but their existence was still precarious, in fact, tragic.

Flavio had survived despite the Catacumba doctor's prediction seventeen years before, and he was healthy, striving, and still full of love. But it looked as if he had gone as far as he could go in his lifetime. Now that his life had been saved, I hoped that he would not waste it chasing a futile dream.

Attempting to escape these depressing thoughts, I opened the package Flavio had given me that afternoon. Inside there was a handsome black billfold, in it a note saying "Happy Father's Day, Gordon. We love you." "Dear Cleuza. Dear Flavio," I thought. A small photograph fell from the billfold into my hand. It was of Flavio Junior astride his scooter bike, wearing a red playsuit. The resemblance to his father was extraordinary. I took out the old *Life* magazine and found the photograph of Flavio lying on the crumpled bed. Placed side by side, the boys in the two pictures looked to be the same person. I stared at the two faces for several moments, realizing suddenly now what the point of Flavio's story was—it lay in this boy, in his alert brown eyes and in his strong, healthy body. Little Flavio had escaped to the top rung of an invisible ladder leading up from the mire of poverty and misery. Neither his body nor his brain would be hampered by the disease and malnutrition that had plagued his father—this father, who all his life would give love and care to his family. With such a start there was no reason that Flavio Junior should not outgrow and outlive the ever-growing Catacumbas of South America.

We were banking northward now, climbing high out over the sea. Down in the darkness below, on the road to Guadalupe, went José, Cleuza, Isabel, and Flavio—he with his hopes tied once more to mine. Perhaps another miracle wasn't as far-fetched as it seemed. It was Flavio's enobling spirit that rallied thousands of people to save him and eventually his son; it was his courage that made millions of others more acutely aware of the tragedy of Catacumba and countless other favelas, barrios, and ghettos like it throughout the world. That spirit, that courage, still compels him. He, and what is born to him, is the future.

New York
June 12, 1977